BESIDE ME

BESIDE ME

A Spiritual Journey in Trust

NIREL

Copyright © 2016 Nirel.

All rights reserved. No part of this book may be used or reproduced by any means, graphic, electronic, or mechanical, including photocopying, recording, taping or by any information storage retrieval system without the written permission of the author except in the case of brief quotations embodied in critical articles and reviews.

Actual events are true. However, all names and places have been changed.

Archway Publishing books may be ordered through booksellers or by contacting:

Archway Publishing
1663 Liberty Drive
Bloomington, IN 47403
www.archwaypublishing.com
1 (888) 242-5904

Because of the dynamic nature of the Internet, any web addresses or links contained in this book may have changed since publication and may no longer be valid. The views expressed in this work are solely those of the author and do not necessarily reflect the views of the publisher, and the publisher hereby disclaims any responsibility for them.

Any people depicted in stock imagery provided by Thinkstock are models, and such images are being used for illustrative purposes only. Certain stock imagery © Thinkstock.

ISBN: 978-1-4808-3237-4 (sc)
ISBN: 978-1-4808-3239-8 (hc)
ISBN: 978-1-4808-3238-1 (e)

Library of Congress Control Number: 2016908818

Print information available on the last page.

Archway Publishing rev. date: 06/10/2016

Contents

Prologue vii
Chapter 1   The Early Years 1
Chapter 2   Marriage 14
Chapter 3   Troubles Begin 22
Chapter 4   Parenting Woes 38
Chapter 5   Troubles Escalate 43
Chapter 6   Real Trouble 63
Chapter 7   The Long Journey 80
Chapter 8   Arrival 102
Chapter 9   New Beginnings 112
Chapter 10 Will Journeys Never End? 134
Chapter 11 Moves, Moves, Moves 174
Chapter 12 The Walk 186
Epilogue 199
Afterword 205

PROLOGUE

Why I Wrote This Book

THIS IS A BOOK BASED on the facts of my life, delivered to the best of my recollection. From my personal journey and study of the Bible, I have learned that we are charged to share the message of how God has worked in our lives. So I'm writing down my experiences here.

What follows is a revelation of the trials and tribulations I've faced, often having nothing but faith to see me through those crises. If one person can see herself (or himself) in these pages and is inspired to change personal behavior, seek help to escape an abusive relationship, explore nagging spiritual emptiness, or better her or his life in any way, then I will have accomplished something—with God's help—beyond anything I could have ever imagined.

Not long ago, my mom and I were talking about some of the things I'd been through (or survived), and she said, "You should write a journal. So I did … periodically. As time marched on, I related some of the passages to friends. The recurring refrain became "You should write a book!" Eventually, that message sunk in, and I began this effort. But I didn't magically sit down one day and write every word and paragraph herein.

It was a journal. I had the basic theme but no idea about where to begin undertaking a book project. However, God places people in your path when you need them for help, inspiration, comfort, or any number of reasons.

How does that work?

A few years ago at a jazz concert, I met a writer who had written twelve books. He was no stranger; I'd met him and his wife through the local jazz society. But until that day, I had no idea that he was an author. I began to tell him about my outline, and he encouraged me to finish my book because it sounded quite interesting and could perhaps be a good seller. He offered to give me some pointers when the story was more developed. So I set to the task and developed my journal into more of a cohesive story. Four months later, I asked my new mentor to look it over.

It was a beautiful fall day when my husband and I visited this gentleman and his wife (both in their eighties) and gave him the completed part of my fledgling manuscript to read. They lived on a large boat in the Gulf of Mexico. (Now, that's character enough for anyone, but octogenarians?) It was amazing to see how these folks embraced life and continued to enjoy it aboard their boat home.

As soon as we were aboard, his phone rang. A mutual friend from the jazz society announced that she and her husband were in the area. Another call followed almost immediately; again, another jazz society friend would be joining us. An impromptu party was then in full swing.

We were talking about how we all ended up at our friends' place; when it was my turn, I told the group that I had made an appointment to be there. They asked, "Why would you make an appointment?" Well, you can just imagine the questions that began flowing when I told them about my manuscript. So I was further encouraged by all and delved, with renewed purpose and energy, into the process.

I had no idea that undertaking the writing of a memoir would be so much work or that I would hit creative droughts. When I faced these troubles, I prayed to my heavenly Father to ask him for help (as I have throughout my life), and he most always answered (though in his time and not mine).

You see, the Lord doesn't always blast a lightning bolt from the sky with a ribbon-wrapped solution directly into your hand. His help is often revealed almost invisibly in the slow ebb and flow of life. Sometimes he delivers quickly though. As an example, I was struggling with how to find a reputable publisher. At a hotel where my husband John and I were staying, I was sitting at a table across from another couple. A little voice told me to talk to them, so I did. I learned that they owned a Christian bookstore and were in town for a conference. When I said I was writing a book based on my Christian faith, the wife could not get to our table fast enough. I told her how God, his angels, and Jesus were always beside me in times of need. I said that if my story could help one person, then my efforts would have been successful. I told her that some of the proceeds from the book will be donated to a charity (or charities) that help abused women. She gave me the contact information for four publishers and said that I could use her name as a reference. Boom! Lightning bolt and ribbon-wrapped answer.

At a recent Monday morning prayer group, someone asked how my book was coming along. I told her about having met the couple who owned a Christian bookstore. My problem was that I had made great progress with my manuscript but that it desperately needed editing, and funds were tight. Hearing that, one of the members piped up and said she knew a person who would graciously help with the editing. We met, and she has proven to be an angel from heaven, and we worked together well on this project. But a year later, she had to abandon the project because of work-related scheduling reasons.

Was this end-game? No. The Lord provided another editor almost immediately—an experienced, retired author and newspaper editor who was eager for something to do. A simple prayer for help, offered in faith, resulted in an answer that was better than expected.

Halfway to completion, I hit a wrong key on my computer and accidentally deleted the entire book and then emptied the trash. *Gone!* My husband was away on business and couldn't imagine how to retrieve the information but suggested I visit the electronics store where the computer was purchased for assistance. The patient sales clerk couldn't help; it was gone forever.

In a panic, I next visited the store's service department and met with the same answer, but an angel must have been listening to my prayers and to that conversation. Another technician overheard and said, "We might try this" (some technical thing), and voilà—I had my book back. A coincidence? I think not. The store staff explained the value of backing up data, and I began performing that process on an almost daily basis.

What follows is the story of my life and how God has been beside me throughout that journey. Hopefully, you will enjoy the story, and you can take something from it or share it with someone who might.

I am patiently waiting to see what the Lord is going to do. Enjoy!

Chapter 1

The Early Years

UNTIL LATE IN LIFE, I did not read the Bible. Nor did I even consider myself a person of faith. Looking back, I've discovered that God's grace has been an amazing part of my entire journey, and I have learned that the Bible is the best place to find knowledge, wisdom, and the answers to questions in life. As you read this story, I hope you will see how I have come to recognize God's presence, protection, and promise.

On June 14, 1949, at four pounds, ten ounces and fourteen inches, I slipped into the world in a relatively simple birth that was a relief for Mom. My brother, Hamilton, had been a very hard delivery. Because I was so small, I couldn't be taken home immediately but remained in the hospital for two weeks, until I reached five pounds.

At that time, Mom and Dad were renting a small apartment, but they were hoping to buy their first home. They found, just as they had dreamed, an affordable wartime house in a nice neighborhood. Then they set to the task of purchasing it. Dad spent two hours at the housing corporation office to see if he would qualify for the $2,500 loan required. He needed $250 for a down payment.

After a couple of hours of stalling, the officials finally called him into the office. They asked if he had been injured in the war. Dad answered, "I was wounded three times and have shrapnel in one leg. Does that count?" The next question was about children. Again, he answered, "Yes. My wife is pregnant with our second child." Each time they asked him something, he had the correct answer.

When the loan was approved, the payments were $25 a month, including taxes, principal, and interest. Four years later, my parents decided that the family had outgrown our small home; they sold it and purchased one that they would retire in.

In February 1953, a new brick bungalow cost my parents $9,500, at $49 a month. My parents bought that house, and Dad, at ninety, still lives there today. It was wintertime in Ontario, and I can vividly remember going by sleigh to see our new home. Later that spring, we moved in.

Shortly after moving into our new home, my friend Jewel was visiting, and I said, "Let's go visit my aunt who lives downtown by the library." When we arrived, we sat on her step giggling. My curious aunt had to investigate what was going on and was amazed when she saw us. The walk to her doorstep was about a mile, and we were only four years old. (I can't remember if we got into trouble.)

It was a great time and place to grow up in. The town's population was around 40,000 then. A park was just down the road, next to a meandering river. The park had a small beach and a tree with a swinging rope that propelled us out into the river. All the kids in the area made full use of the swing by taking a running start, leaping on the rope, swinging out over the water, and then letting go, falling into the cold, refreshing river.

Our group of tightly-knit neighborhood friends was always together. We spent every possible minute outdoors. My memories of tagging along with my brother and his friends to find just the right place to build a tree fort, and the days spent doing that, are some of my best recollections. We'd spend our days and evenings playing all manner of games. Some of my favorites were red rover and hide-and-seek; I also loved just frolicking outside after dark.

When television became widely available, my parents were among the first in our neighborhood to buy one. Because we were so blessed, Mom would have all our friends over to watch TV and serve us popcorn and soda. I remember watching *Howdy Doody, Captain Kangaroo,* and *Bozo the Clown* with our circle of friends.

When I wanted to be alone, I'd push my baby buggy to the park … by myself. I would put my dolly in the baby swing, and I'd take her up the steps of the "big" slide. Then down we would go, thrilled with the speed of the drop. Because I was so small, going up there was exciting for me. Being up on that slide gave me a different perspective from what I was used to daily. I could look down at things instead of always looking up.

My poor big brother had to drag his little sister everywhere. On Saturdays, the gang took the bus downtown to see King Kong or Frankenstein or John Wayne movies at the local theater. My first recollection of one of those trips was when I was six. I distinctly remember the bus fare being five cents and the cost of admission to the theater a whopping ten cents. Those days were wonderful. The fear of someone trying to kidnap kids was the furthest thing from anyone's mind.

One cold winter day during the school year, we experienced a blizzard. The wind came really fast, and snow accumulated at an alarming rate. School was released at lunch, and as I walked out the door, the principal saw me literally blown off the sidewalk. Concerned, he walked beside me to protect me from the wind and to make certain I arrived home safely. Though I was eight years old, my physical size was that of a much smaller child. The principal told Mom to keep me home the rest of the day. Mom and I had a great time together. We watched a movie and prepared the evening meal for the rest of the family.

Several years later, I was on my way home from school again for lunch. The early spring weather had turned bitterly cold. Freezing rain had begun early that morning, and the roads were very icy. I was crossing at an intersection when a car stopped to pick up children. Just then, I slipped. I was so small for a ten-year-old that I slid right under the car. I don't think the driver even realized what happened, and I wasn't going to find out the hard way. To avoid being run over I got out from under that car before it started moving again. Thank God!

On Friday nights, my mom and I watched *Alfred Hitchcock*. I can almost taste the root beer and popcorn that was part of our weekly ritual. What fun she and I had! Being with Mom every Friday night was, and remains, a special memory.

Home life wasn't always fun. Dad drank to block out his horrific memories of war. Today, therapists have a name for it—post-traumatic stress disorder. Back then, you just dealt with it the best you could. During those trying times, my mother hid a lot of the grief brought on by Dad's condition.

I remember a story Mom told me when I was in my teens. Mom and Dad had met before the war, but Dad wouldn't marry her because he knew he would be going overseas and into battle. He didn't want to leave her a widow. Out of her love for Dad, Mom went to services and prayed a specific novena for several consecutive weeks, asking God to bring him back from the front. God heard her plea.

One night following her nightly prayers, my mother received a vision of a battlefield. Two men walked toward her while the battle raged around them. She learned later that through all the many battles they encountered, Dad and his best friend were the only two soldiers to survive out of an entire regiment.

In later years, our mom would pray those same novenas, asking the Lord to keep our family together. Those prayers were also answered.

One time, we were coming home from my aunt's house, which was about a two-hour drive from home. We had gone to support her (Mom's sister) after she called to say my uncle and she were divorcing. It was around nine o'clock at night. I remember the weather had turned from a light snow to a wet mess, with big flakes that made the roads very slippery. We were going down a hill when the car spun out, went off the road, and slid down the edge of a bank into a deep snowdrift. We thought no one would be on that stretch of country road that time of night. Our thoughts were grim, but I know Mom was praying just as hard as I was.

In the next few minutes, a car came and stopped halfway down the hill. Two drunks got out of the car. One of them fell and slid the rest of the way down the hill. We all laughed as he asked, "Are you waiting for a train?" The two men moved our car back onto the road as if it were a toy. In no time at all, we were back in the car and headed for home. With another forty miles to go, Mom and I prayed all the way. Arriving safely, we were very thankful to God for sending two of the most unlikely angels to help us that night.

I was twelve the next year when we went on a family camping trip to Canada's east coast. After driving for hours, my dad felt tired and decided to go to a beach for a break and a swim. We saw no access to the ocean, but Dad spotted a narrow dirt road heading in the right direction and took advantage of it. What he didn't know was that it was a railway access, and it only went as far as the tracks, beyond which there was no more roadway.

Dad started to cross the tracks before he realized that the road had ended, and the front tires found nothing but air. There we teetered, with no ground beneath us, stuck on the railroad tracks. We had no way to back up and no road to go forward on. Exhausted, Dad told us to put on our bathing suits, we would worry about the car later.

After we'd enjoyed the beach and the frigid water of the North Atlantic, we all set out to look for driftwood and anything else we could put under the car's tires to gain some purchase. With the whole family's participation, in what seemed like no time at all, we obtained enough wood to get the job done.

Putting everything we'd gathered under the car, we eventually built a pile that made the newly-raised road level with the track. Dad was able to back the car off the railroad track with no damage. Believe it or not, within minutes of getting the car moved, a train came rolling down the rails. Another angel was beside us that day.

The very next night, we couldn't find an available camping spot. We looked until well after dark, but all the camps were taken. Around ten o'clock that night, Dad just pulled over and set up camp. By that time, it was pitch black, and we had no opportunity to check our surroundings. When morning came, we awakened from a much-needed rest but couldn't help noticing an odor in the air. We'd set up camp right beside a garbage dump; and the tent was pitched uncomfortably close to the edge of a cliff. We couldn't get out of there fast enough!

At that point in my life, I frequently experienced swelling and soreness around my knee. In fact, I'd missed a good number of school days because of the problem. That summer, God healed my knee.

Mom's relatives lived in French Canada—one of our stopovers that year. At a shrine we visited, Mom and I watched a man go into the church with crutches and come out walking normally. We watched as he hung his crutches beside many canes, wheelchairs, walkers, and other devices. Mom asked me to go and pray and ask God to cure my knee. I did what she requested and haven't had a single experience of water on the knee since. I believed God would heal me. I had no doubt, and to this day—decades later—I give thanks to God for answering my prayer.

Time moved on, and eventually I turned sweet sixteen. My closest friend at that time was Carissa, and she remains one of my closest friends today.

We were inseparable as teens. One evening, the two of us decided to walk downtown. We met three guys whom Carissa knew from her school. They asked us if we'd like to join them. I said no, but Carissa said it would be okay and not to worry. That was a huge mistake. Instinct told me something was fishy. I knew it immediately, even at the tender (and stupid) age of sixteen. Looking back, it makes me shudder to think about what could have happened.

The guys drove us to a lake where a small boat was tied up. They insisted on taking the rowboat to a cabin out on an island. All my alarms went off, and I started praying to our Father in heaven for help. Their stolen rowboat started to sink, and we all jumped out of it. The boys pulled it back to shore and put it back where they had found it. They were desperate to get us to that small piece of land surrounded by water, and one of the guys spotted a bigger boat to steal. Guess what? That boat was chained up and locked. Frustrated, they gave up and drove us back to town. I told Carissa never to put me in such a dangerous situation again.

The year we graduated, I became a beautician and moved on, as did Carissa. Dating was not the greatest experience for me. My choices in men were a problem early on. Looking back on it, I think it may have been because I didn't pray and ask for God's help in the matter. I just figured the right one would eventually come across my radar.

Those hit-or-miss choices proved to be poor ones. Later in life, I met some mature adult women at church and discovered the Lord's way of choosing a mate. They had taken Bible studies in their youth and were taught to pray for Christian companions. Their husbands seemed to be good men, and though they may have had problems, none were serious. And no one in this group had ever hinted at divorce.

In 1967, I thought I'd met the man for me. Charlie was a neat and well-behaved gentleman. He opened the car door for me; he treated me in a special way and catered to my every desire. He even helped me take care of my sisters when I was babysitting. But after dating him for two years, my gut was telling me that something wasn't right.

Having graduated from cosmetology school in Ontario, I began to make arrangements to go to

Michigan to live with friends of my parents and to earn my license in cosmetology there. Those friends owned two salons and ran a cosmetology school; so, in my mind, it was a terrific opportunity.

My aunt confided that my mom was praying for God to help me see the potential danger of living in a city steeped in crime. After all, I was a sheltered girl from a very small city in southern Ontario and wasn't very street-smart. Who knows what could happen to a naive little girl from Canada?

The time away would have given me an opportunity to see if Charlie was the one I should marry, but Mom got her wish (be careful what you pray for), and I never got that chance.

The first time Charlie and I went downtown together, we encountered a male friend of mine. Afterward, Charlie became very jealous, and I thought: *Boy, does he ever care for me! Isn't that sweet? He loves me so much!* I wish I had known better. Now I know that jealousy is one sign of manipulation and control. As time goes on, the situation only gets worse, not better—not ever.

I was supposed to be in Michigan in August but found out in July that I was pregnant. My dream was shattered. I confess that I considered having an abortion but decided against it. Somehow, I knew in my heart that this was going to be a very special event in our lives. Today, I know that all babies are a gift. I know that some women, who desperately want to, can't have babies. So I'm very thankful for Mulligan, my son.

Chapter 2

Marriage

On the hottest day of August, Charlie and I were married. I swear that the temperature was in the high nineties that fateful day. The wedding was to be at eight o'clock in the evening on Friday night, Labor Day weekend. Due to the heavy traffic, the maid of honor, the best man, and even the groom were all late. The wedding took place at a Catholic church. At that time, no one could get married after nine o'clock in the evening. Just minutes before nine, we heard tires squealing in the parking lot, and the wedding party arrived. I must say that during the delay, I gave a lot of thought to not marrying Charlie. But in the end, I went ahead with it.

The priest asked if we would like to postpone the ceremony until the next day, and we looked around and saw family and friends already there. Postponing meant everyone would have to come back the next day, so we both said no. It must have been one of the fastest Catholic weddings in the history of the church. Around eleven o'clock, Charlie and I left the party our parents put on for us. We headed off for the best honeymoon spot in Ontario.

Not far outside the city, we had car problems and had to get a motel close by. Thank goodness for that because Charlie no sooner got into bed than he passed out from drinking and partying. Oh well, so much for that.

Cliché as it may be, the honeymoon took place in Niagara Falls. We rode on a tour bus and then walked under a grand waterfall. We were given bright yellow rain coats with boots to match. Overlooking this great natural wonder and seeing the roaring force of water falling onto the rocks below, how could we not believe in our maker?

The next day, we went to museums and took in the sights. After three days, our honeymoon ended. Charlie had to get back to work because he had just started his new job.

After the wedding, we moved from our home town to a large metropolitan city where Charlie found work. During the Christmas season, he had a week off. We were back in our home town to be with our families for Christmas. We stayed a few days with my parents and then moved on to visit with his family for the remainder of our trip.

During our holiday visit, we'd made plans to visit one of Charlie's friends for an early New Year's dinner celebration (the date was December thirtieth). When we arrived, Charlie's friend told me that it looked like I'd be having the baby sooner rather than later. Having delivered three children of her own, she knew from experience that my birthing signs were strong.

When dinner was served, I ate like a vulture. I just couldn't seem to get enough to eat. We returned to Charlie's parent's home around midnight and went straight to bed. Around one o'clock in the morning, I was suddenly awakened by severe cramping. Thinking I had indigestion from the quantity of food I'd devoured, I didn't want to wake anyone up—not even Charlie.

By three o'clock, the pains had subsided substantially and were now just a minor nagging in my lower back, like a menstrual pain. However, because they were occurring regularly (every five minutes, like clockwork), I was concerned and woke Charlie. He went to tell his mother what was going on; while he was gone, I experienced a sensation that I can only describe as something dropping out of me. I was later told that my mucus plug had come out.

When Charlie told his mother what was happening, she came and said, "Just put your coat and boots on over your night clothes and get to the hospital. Don't change because the doctor will likely want to see what has come out of you. They'll send your clothes home with Charlie." Even I was wondering and a little worried about what had happened.

I'm not aware of anything else that was said or even what I was thinking at that moment in time. But I do recall when we went out to get into the car, it was bitter cold. The night sky was perfectly clear—clearer than I can remember ever having seen it before or since. It seemed as though I could see every star.

At this early hour, the town's people were all safely tucked in their beds (keeping warm, no doubt), so the streets were absolutely quiet. I don't recall seeing a single car on our trip to the hospital. Apprehensive and scared, I wanted to stall for time, but the trip took only minutes because the hospital was close by. In a small city, a person can get anywhere fairly quickly.

Looking back on it all, I have to admit that I was not at all prepared for childbirth. Even though I had taken prenatal classes, I was fast realizing that it was all foreign to me. The other mothers in my class were doctors' wives and seemed to know everything already. Not wanting to seem ignorant by asking too many questions, I just went with the flow and remained quiet. Freezing my tush off in that car, heading for the hospital and the inevitable event that was about to take place, I wished I'd asked a lot more questions!

Charlie and I arrived at the hospital at about four o'clock in the morning. A close neighbor of my parents happened to be the head nurse on duty that night. A few years earlier, I'd been her children's babysitter. She didn't recognize me by my married name, but as soon as she saw me, she was truly surprised to find her skinny, 103-pound, five-foot-tall babysitter about to have a baby of her own.

Still in a state of relative comfort, except for the regularly occurring minor back pain, I asked her if my baby was really on its way or if I should I go back home to bed? By that time, I'd been awake since midnight; I was really tired. Then I asked her why the baby's head was still pointed upward. She told me it was the other way around; the baby had turned. She said I wasn't going home or anywhere else for that matter. She instructed me that the nurses would be back soon to prep me; she finished with the statement, "This baby is really on its way."

When determining the projected date for a baby's arrival in those days, I think the doctors went mostly by the last menstrual cycle. For no apparent reason, my cycles became erratic every spring. I even missed complete cycles. This odd occurrence caused me to lose track of my schedule. Using what information I could provide in the early stages of my pregnancy, I was told that Mulligan would be born on the first of February.

Mulligan hadn't been told of the schedule and arrived the morning of December thirty-first, weighing seven pounds and fifteen ounces. Missed it by a month!

The Lord blessed me during the birth of my son. He was a very easy birth—a breeze coming into this world. Honestly and fortunately, my birthing pain was minimal. When the baby's head was coming out, I asked for painkillers—mainly because of all the horrid stories I had heard. I thought my pains were the beginning of my labor, but the truth was that Mulligan was already out of the birth canal and into the world.

When I held him in my arms later that afternoon, I wondered how, seven months earlier, I could have ever thought about having an abortion. He was beautiful and wondrous, with the most perfect skin color and the cutest chubby cheeks. Charlie and I were so proud to be parents of a baby boy. The family name could be passed on with pride. Thank you, Father in heaven, for giving me a healthy baby who would become a wonderful son.

Mulligan was a big, healthy baby. I'm very small-framed, so if he'd been any bigger, I wouldn't have been able to give birth naturally. (Just before delivery, I weighed only 103 pounds.) He had beautiful blue eyes and reddish hair. Later, it turned to a light golden blond, and now it is dark brown. He is quite handsome, if I say so myself. He has his dad's good looks.

Charlie was exhausted and needed to get some rest. He had just started a new job and had to be ready for work on Monday. Our apartment in the city was a few hours away from our parents, so he really had no choice but to leave the two of us behind in their care. He would come for us the following weekend.

When Mulligan and I left the hospital, we stayed with my mom and dad at their home. That first night, I decided to stay up and wait for Mulligan to cry in case I did not hear him. By the time he woke up, it was past five in the morning, and I was exhausted. Thank goodness, my mom came in to feed him. She had already warmed the baby bottle. I may have been a good babysitter, but I was quite a novice at being a mother.

Today, books on giving birth and child rearing are plentiful. New mothers can use the Internet to find information about becoming a mom. But back in 1969, we had only our family, friends, and our community. Today's new mothers don't have to heat baby bottles or mix formulas. We made it through though. I learned what I needed to know, and Mulligan grew stronger every day. The following weekend, Charlie came for us, and we went home to the city.

Two months later in our apartment, I was cleaning the outlet on the stove with a wet cloth and a knife. Suddenly, the knife slipped into the socket! I realized I could not let go. I could have been electrocuted that day, but God's hand was on me. Another angel was beside me. I got on my knees to thank God for my life because Mulligan would have been in his crib all day with nothing to eat or drink. Charlie would have come home and found me on the floor with a screaming baby in his bed.

Chapter 3

Troubles Begin

Before my son was three months old, I was going down stairs with him in my arms. When I missed the first step, with a horrible yell I tumbled down fifteen marble steps. Mulligan was fine because he ended up on top of me. All I had was a scrape on my arm. Another angel was at my side.

The following year found me troubled. Charlie was not working and didn't seem interested in finding work. Money was very tight at one point. Charlie's dad helped him get a job, but Charlie didn't like taking the bus to and from work, so he quit that job. This troubled me, but I kept my mouth shut. Following several months of Charlie's unemployment, I told our parents I was planning to move about 1,500 miles west to a city in which two of my sisters were living.

I was fed up with Charlie not working and his lack of ambition even to look for work.

The following week, we moved back to our home town. His father, an executive with a major corporation, managed to get Charlie a job at his plant. I thought my problems would end there, but that wasn't the case.

By that time, our son was two. I took him to parks and to the beach where I played as a child. I met a woman there who also had a two-year-old and who became a friend. As we spent more time together, I realized that she had also married a man who was just like Charlie.

Somehow, it was easier for me to look at her life and see a fast-developing picture of marital destruction. For some reason beyond my comprehension, I found it difficult to focus on my own situation. Watching and listening to her life, however, reflected what was happening in my own life like a mirror. The reflection was not a pretty one. I only wish now that I could have seen the signs before marrying him, but Charlie, like her husband, fit the profile of a controller and heavy drinker. Looking back, I knew after the first evening of the honeymoon that I had gotten myself into a bad situation.

As time passed, Charlie was frequently absent from his job. His most common excuse was back pain, and maybe it was real, but there was a very predictable pattern to his misery. It mysteriously manifested itself on a Friday morning or a Sunday night.

Life wasn't all bad. Charlie's mom and dad helped us buy our first home by providing us with the money for a down payment. Because they had helped Charlie's siblings with similar financial gifts, I assumed that it was an act of generosity. But from prior experience, I should have known better. I learned that the down payment was being loaned to us at the going rate of 7 percent interest.

I say that I should have known better because early in our marriage, I had a strange experience with Charlie's parents. Once, at our first apartment (before we'd moved back to our home town), his parents came to our place for Easter dinner. At that time, we didn't have a broom or a dustpan. So when his parents arrived, they gave me a new broom and a dustpan. Or so I thought! When they gave me the "gift," Charlie's dad asked me for $1.07, saying that it was just to keep me honest! I felt terrible and thereafter considered them to be my "outlaws."

There were frequent layoffs at Charlie's workplace, and I wasn't bringing in any money. So I decided to get a job in my chosen profession as a beautician. In no time at all, I secured a part-time position and began contributing to the family budget. But Charlie's work remained sporadic, with layoffs and his "back pain."

During an extended period of no work (six months) that meant his unemployment would soon run out, I asked Charlie to go back to school. The government offered courses to help unemployed people. When he refused, I told him we were going to have to move out of our small home town, where work opportunities were limited, to a place where he could more readily find work. He opted to go to school.

Trusting soul that I am, I fully expected that out of concern for his young family Charlie would faithfully attend his classes. Because of his irregular attendance, however, I soon suspected something wasn't quite right. Then one day, Charlie and his attractive female teacher appeared in the mall where I worked. To make the situation look good, two other classmates were with them. This seemed strange because they were all supposed to be in class. Intuition told me that something was very wrong with this picture.

Later that same day, one of the classmates from his school came back to the shop and confided that she thought the teacher was after my Charlie. I said then,

"Spouses can't be taken away unless, in their minds and hearts, they've already left."

Soon after that, we attended the graduation ceremony of the school's program. When we arrived, Charlie told me he had lost a bet; as a consequence, he had to take the teacher out to dinner. Who was I to make a scene? What choice did I have? I already knew that he was going—no matter what I felt about it. But to know the person I lived with was courting someone else was especially painful, particularly as I realized that he was also shirking his marriage and family responsibilities.

Later that same evening, the teacher's younger brother asked me out. I was tempted to pay Charlie back but decided that two wrongs don't make a right. I refused his offer. Saying "no" was especially hard because he was a looker.

During casual conversation with Charlie's teacher, the subject of dating came up. Charlie's teacher announced that her brother would never date an older woman. Boy was she in for a surprise! I let her know what had just taken place.

Over time, it became Charlie's habit to go out just after supper Tuesday nights. He said that he was going shopping, but when he arrived home, he never had a bag or package. I did question him about it because any other day of the week Charlie wasn't a shopper. In time, he also established another night out—race night—with his friends. So I started going out with my girlfriends. We would go out to dinner and to the local pub and enjoy a couple of drinks and finger food. This became our version of girl's night out. At that point in our lives, Mulligan was about eleven years old.

After a year of idleness and play, Charlie finally got back to work. Shortly thereafter, he started hanging around with a group of guys from work. Because I was told that they were going to the nearby horse racing track, I called them "the gamblers." Later, I learned that the three of them did occasionally go to the races, but at least one of them (we'll call him Sam) was a swinger. I discovered this fact when we went to a Christmas party at Sam's home. Being clueless and trusting, I had no idea what was going on. But as soon as we stepped inside their home, Sam's wife led the way to their downstairs recreation room and said she and Charlie were going to dance. I had to laugh because, you see, Charlie was never a dancer! Charlie, Sam, and Sam's wife had worked out a plan in advance. I was the only one unaware of the plan.

Not even five minutes had passed before they were dancing very slowly and close together. This was not the dance of total strangers but of persons well acquainted with each other. Thirty minutes later, some guests actually said they thought the two of them were a married couple.

I retaliated by playing up to Sam. Because I played the role of homemaker so well and because Sam was catering to my every whim (something he never did for his wife), I'm certain that some people thought I was his wife, and I'm certain that he thought he was well on his way to obtaining the goal of seduction.

They had planned it out in advance. Ignorant of that plan, I was inwardly seething and seeking vengeance.

Naive, trusting, and innocent, I was about to crash. I joined the men for jokes and drinks while the wives chatted; I hadn't seen Charlie for some time. I went looking for him, and I found him before long. He was coming out of the fruit cellar with Sam's wife. Obviously, they hadn't been dancing. I demanded that we leave immediately.

The very next week, I awoke about four o'clock in the morning. I went to the window and saw a van in front of our home where our car was normally parked. In the morning, I asked Charlie where the van came from and where our car was. He told me a friend needed to borrow our car and gave Charlie the van to get home in. Stupidly, I believed him. Many years later, I figured it out; Charlie needed the van to facilitate his own pleasures.

Another year passed, and Christmas was coming, along with another party. But this time, the gathering was for Charlie's work, so I agreed to go. Charlie became quite drunk; at some point during the party, he went missing, leaving me with "the gambler" gang with whom we'd been seated. What a mistake! They said we'd go look for him after everyone had eaten, but I was in a panic, thinking the worst.

I had left my purse and money at home, thinking I wouldn't need them at a party. So I couldn't call a cab. I looked around and saw friends of my parents. I politely asked them if they would give me a ride. They could see how distressed I was and had already seen how inebriated Charlie was. Off we went to look for my drunken husband.

Our home backed onto the canal and a river was just down the street. If Charlie had decided to walk home, my fear was that he might have somehow fallen into the water and drowned. After an unsuccessful search, my parents' friends drove me home. I learned from that experience to always have my purse and some money with me. Had I been prepared, I could have taken a taxi.

The gamblers had acted strangely after Charlie left, trying to keep me there at the party. When I arrived home, my babysitter let me in, and I waited until about two in the morning before going to bed. Around four or five in the morning, Charlie came rolling in. Years later, I'd figured out that Charlie had left with another woman. How stupid and naive I was back then.

The next morning, I suffered because I asked Charlie where he had gone. I demanded to know what he did after leaving me the night before. He had no answer but accused me of having an affair. Then he hit me in the eye.

By afternoon, I had a serious shiner. When I showed up for work on Monday morning with my eye black and blue, the girls asked what door I had walked into. It wasn't the first time they had seen me like that (with bruises on my arms). For the first time, however, I told the truth, which proved to be a pivotal moment in taking control of my life.

Previously, I had hidden the truth about Charlie's abuse because I was ashamed. I had kept this secret from everyone for years—even my family and closest friends.

Recently I learned that drinkers frequently accuse their partners of having extramarital affairs. In his attempt to manipulate me, Charlie went so far as to check my mail and intercept my phone messages without telling me who had called. These were attempts to maintain control over me and to protect his secrets.

About that time, we had a pool installed in our backyard. Up to that point, our summertime weekends involved trips to Charlie's parents' lake cottage, which should have been a lot of fun but usually meant spending most of our time doing chores and housework. When I wasn't working at my job, this wasn't a problem; I love to help out. However, I was then working full time at a job that required two twelve-hour shifts in any workweek and keeping house too. I loved my job, but a little rest after a long week at work would have been appreciated.

Being asked to my in-laws' cottage for long weekends meant helping get the boats out of the water, cleaning the bottoms, tidying the cottage, turning over mattresses, and washing windows. Weekends at the cottage were always a lot of work. That was reason enough to purchase our own pool.

For these reasons and because Mulligan was coming into his teenage years—trying years for any parent—I believed we'd have a better idea about the kids he was hanging out with, where he was, and what he was doing if they were swimming together at our house.

He was a social boy with many friends, and the pool was heaven for them all.

I paid for that pool. Though I didn't know it at the time, a great portion of Charlie's earnings were going to another vice—gambling. Looking back now, I understand what a fool he made of me again. The gamblers or his work friends would gamble during their lunch hour and do even more serious betting at the track. I understand now where his paychecks were really going.

Initially, we all enjoyed the pool. Before long though, Charlie invited his friends and buddies from work and the neighborhood. On any given Saturday (and sometimes on Sundays), they would come over for a swim and then drink all afternoon. I soon realized the pool was becoming a big problem.

Mulligan had friends stay overnight frequently, and I encouraged him to do this. I wanted him to have a fondness for our home. Oftentimes, there would be four or five friends around. They'd swim until almost midnight and then watch movies. That hour was too late for them to walk home. For all his faults, Charlie is a great cook, and he would cook up great breakfasts for everyone.

In the winter, Mulligan and his buddies would cross-country ski, skate, and play hockey on the canal behind our home. In the spring, they would fish and hike along the pond nearby.

When Mulligan was fourteen years old, we took him and a friend to Ottawa for The Winter Interlude. It was an event that included skating on the miles-long canal, viewing snow sculptures, and passing by vendors selling everything imaginable. We took them to see everything the capital city of Canada had to offer.

I remember one particular morning. At the hotel restaurant, we discovered that Mulligan's friend had never been to a buffet. When we explained the concept of a buffet, his eyes grew as big as saucers. He wanted to know what he was allowed to have, and I am almost certain there wasn't a strip of bacon left after those two teenagers got through.

Sometimes Mulligan and I would go for bike rides and even shop together. One particular spring day, my son's friend, a girl, seemed out of sorts when she saw us together in the mall. She didn't realize that I was his mother and thought that I was his new girlfriend. Even though I wasn't a teenage mother, until I was in my early forties, people frequently had a hard time believing that I was Mulligan's mother and not his sister.

While Mulligan and I were forming a bond, the marital abuse continued. The crazy logic associated with drunkenness, gambling, and physical and mental abuse (and trying to keep it all secret) was a source of constant, escalating stress for me. One of my outlets or sanity checks was to clean house. You could eat off the floors or out of the toilets; I sometimes scrubbed them until two o'clock in the morning. Even though times were rough emotionally, God provided me with solid friends.

Marley came into my life one day at work. Through the course of our conversation, we discovered that she and her husband and Charlie and I liked to cross-country ski. She and I talked about the things we enjoyed and found that we had many similar interests. She and her husband took us to see a Neil Diamond movie and afterwards came back to our place for coffee and dessert. That evening, we made plans to go cross-country skiing and have dinner with them a few weeks later. That was the beginning of a long-standing relationship, a true friendship still to this day.

In the winter, the four of us would go nearly every other weekend to a resort not far from home. We would eat a buffet luncheon and later use the inn's well-groomed cross-country ski trails. The paths took us deep into the woods. At the halfway point, the resort had set out a circle of logs so that people could sit and rest. A roaring fire was always ablaze to keep us warm during the interlude, and hot chocolate was available. Not far from where we would sit, the inn had placed a great big salt block for the deer. In the later part of the afternoon on one particular trip, we were treated to the spectacle of six deer feasting on that salt block. Being so close to them was an amazing experience. Like cattle, deer need salt in their diet. Finding a whole herd seeking salt near the roadside in winter is not unusual. The rock salt used to treat snow and ice leaves a residue that deer and moose can easily access.

Those were peaceful, calm, and quiet weekends that seemed more *normal* than the raucous pool weekends that had become our summertime habit. They were times of rest and recovery for my spirit. On another outing, we completed our cross-country journey to find a very special treat of horses hitched to a sleigh. Any guest of the inn could take a sleigh ride through the forest. We surely enjoyed our sleigh ride with two large, well-groomed Clydesdales pulling us—their rhythmic breath frosting in the cold air, their mighty hooves pounding, and their bells ringing out a magical symphony. Newly-fallen snow glistened and sparkled on the ground. We were gliding along in a winter wonderland, a world full of absolute peace. I wonder if the owner of that sleigh knows how much we appreciated his kindness and how that memory has lasted to this day. It was an amazing gift for my troubled spirit. No doubt, God knows our hearts!

The shortest month of the year, February, always seemed long to me. To make that time more pleasurable and pass more quickly, we tried to have a February get-together every year. Remembering the experience of our sleigh ride at the lodge two years earlier and how much fun it was, I decided to create that kind of experience to share with our friends. I hired a man who owned a team of horses and a sleigh and who charged by the hour.

Our party of pals met him at a field outside the city on a stormy winter day in Ontario. With no sunshine peeking through the thick gray storm clouds and the wind driving the bitter cold through our snowsuits (as though we were wearing nothing at all), the cold, blustery winds in our faces made the experience even more intense. The falling snow was blowing sideways, and the fallen snow formed into wicked drifts. We were all bundled up with scarves around our necks; heavy boots and warm mittens were the order of the day. The mighty gusts blew our hats off. But all in all, we had a great time.

About an hour into our adventure, we had to get off the sleigh. The snow had become so deep that the horses were having a hard time pulling us through the snowdrifts. They were so deep that in order to get back onto the sleigh, I needed a big boost. The snow was up to my waist.

We were chilled to the bone. Then the ride was over, and we all headed back to our cars and drove back to our place for a big feast. Everyone brought a special dish. Charlie cooked the meat because everyone loved his chef's style. He really was a great cook. Too bad his drinking nearly destroyed our lives. (More on that later.)

The following February, we hosted an outdoor get- together with our next door neighbors. Our backyards ended at a body of water that froze over in the wintertime, which was great for ice skating. We built a big fire for warmth, and everyone enjoyed cross-country skiing, ice skating, sitting around the fire, or just talking back at the house. Since there was always something to do, the last person didn't leave until nearly three o'clock in the morning.

Chapter 4

Parenting Woes

It was around this time that my son turned sixteen. He was going to a school dance, and I gave him enough money to buy a hamburger, fries, and a drink for himself and his date. He left the house at six o'clock, but by eight we received a call that our son was in bad shape.

We went to the school to see what was wrong. Two big policemen were holding him up. He was so sick he couldn't even stand on his own. We asked if our son was okay, and the police officers advised us to take him to the hospital. Instead of having dinner with the money we'd provided, I learned that the kids had all bought peach schnapps. Mulligan's blood was starting to show signs of alcohol poisoning from lack of food. The so-called friends he was with ignored him and left him in a snow bank in a field, in freezing weather. I was told later that he could have died from exposure had he not been spotted by a bus driver who called the police.

When we arrived at the hospital, I was in such bad shape that I was taken to a private room with a chapel where I could pray for Mulligan. I was beside myself because I had learned I just couldn't trust my teenager. Charlie, who came with me, played it cool of course. I know he was thinking all boys (or most) try this type of stunt. I asked the doctor to check to see if my son had drugs in his system. The physician told me that Mulligan didn't show any signs of drug use. I told my son never to go out again with those kids. Did he obey me? No.

A few months passed, and we received yet another phone call from one of the other mothers. She said her son phoned to say that he and several others, including my son, had been in an accident, and they were walking home. She said she and her husband were going to look for them and that I should wait by the phone in case they called or came to our home.

That first call came at midnight. As the time passed, I did some serious praying. About two o'clock in the morning, Mulligan came through the door unharmed. Thank you, God.

Many problems came with being a parent, but I never received much support from good old Charlie. So on that night, I indeed thanked the Lord for bringing my son home safely. That very night, I gave my son over to God, asking him to watch over Mulligan. Being his mom, I soon realized that I was too young and inexperienced to raise a teenager.

The morning before all this took place; mother superior had come in to get her hair done. I asked her to please take some money I had saved up from tips to give to a charity. I am not saying that I bought my son a second chance in life, but God did spare all the kids in the vehicle that night. The young driver had put the pedal to the metal, and then Mulligan tried to pull the driver's leg off of the gas pedal because no one had seat belts on. My son then threw his arm in front of the girl he was with and held on as they hit a pothole. The truck went high into the air and flipped a few times. The truck had a cap on the back, and a couple was riding in there. When the truck flipped, they were thrown out. The boy was fine, and the girl ended up with only a scratch on her leg.

My dad went to see the wreck and said the truck was a total write-off. He told the boys that the last time he'd seen something like that, the soldiers in the vehicle had all died.

Mulligan's behavior was becoming too big of a problem for me to handle. The next morning, I told my son that it was time to get help. He had disobeyed us, and I was at my wit's end. (I should mention that Mulligan was by then almost six feet tall.) I had a regular client—a priest who had spoken to me about his work in counseling teens. So Charlie and I took Mulligan to see him.

When we arrived, we sat down at a huge antique table. After speaking with the three of us about what was going on, the priest told Charlie and me that he was going upstairs for a private talk with Mulligan. I heard loud noises from upstairs, but I wasn't sure what was happening. I did not understand until later.

After Mulligan returned, he was very quiet and stayed that way for a long while. He just wasn't himself. Over time, when some minor problems arose, I threatened to take him back to the country church. Only then did I learn that the priest had approached him—and not in a good way. He explained the noise I had heard: it was another old table (like the one we were sitting at down below them) scraping across the floor. Thank God that Mulligan was able to protect himself by pulling the table between the priest and himself. These days, that sort of thing has become more exposed and commonplace, but the issue was just surfacing back then. Mulligan handled the situation using his size, and I never again mentioned the subject to him. I took his word only because I heard the movement of the furniture.

Years had passed by the time this all finally came to light. I felt it was too late for me to go to the priest and confront him. I wish now that I had done so because I might have saved other young boys from his unwanted advances.

Chapter 5

Troubles Escalate

ONE EVENING WHEN MULLIGAN WAS nineteen, he was at a friend's house. Charlie called me into Mulligan's room and said, "Let's try something new." I had no idea that I was in for a night of brutal and abusive sex. Being adventurous and without knowing his plan, I agreed to being bound. He rammed into me every which way. I will not go into it in any more detail than to say, "What pain!"

My son came home the next night, and Charlie was upstairs—drunk and asleep as usual for a weekend night. My son asked me why I was crying. I said that for me to keep peace in our family, I must leave. He asked what had happened in his room the other night. I opened up and told him that I'd been hiding my feelings about the abuse and every other bad thing that had happened over the years. I shared only the information about his father that I thought a nineteen-year-old could handle. Mulligan told me that he'd had a gut feeling that something was not right.

I told my son that I was having visions of cracks in the walls and the ceiling and the house caving in on me as our family was being torn apart. I was about to ask for a divorce, and I was blaming myself for what was happening. I had tried so hard to keep our family from falling apart.

Weeks went by, but I'd finally had enough. I went with Charlie for walks in the neighborhood to talk about selling the house. Many of the neighbors probably thought: *Wasn't that sweet for two people to be so in love?* I wonder how they felt just a short time later, hearing the news of our splitting up and moving away.

A few months earlier, I had received a letter from his parents stating that $200 a month, plus interest, for our mortgage payment had not been deposited into their bank account for the last three years. Since there was little left owing on the mortgage, they had paid it off for us, stipulating that their monthly repayments needed to go into their account. Charlie agreed to pay it because my money went for all the other bills. I had asked his family to let me know if the money wasn't deposited into the account. They did—three years later.

I told them that their son was an alcoholic and might be spending the money elsewhere. They did not accept that response. A few weeks later, they sent me another hate-letter, stating that I owed them three years' worth of payments and that their lawyer would be getting in touch with me.

This was all happening in the midst of my planning a beautiful party for their fiftieth wedding anniversary. I had sent out invitations to the mayor and police chief and many more very important friends. These threats were how they returned my kindness.

I went to Charlie to get some money for a bookcase to finish off the living room for the big day. I took the bank book and found there was nothing in the account. I thought there was at least $2,000 in savings. I was in total shock and in tears. I am sorry now for having trusted him and for not having kept track of the account. Thank God, I had my own bank account to pay the bills.

We did have the party, and it was a success. The day was a beautiful, bright day. The backyard had gorgeous flower beds with lovely shrubs and flowers. We arranged for a bouquet of red roses to be placed on the table, and the pool was sparkling. The only problem was my heart, which was heavy with grief. I wanted to make a speech to say I would be divorcing their son but did not want to spoil their day.

Not knowing what to do about my home life, I went into a depression. I didn't eat for five days. I lost weight and except for my work, slept all the time. My neighbor dropped by and found that I'd been in bed all day. I did not know it then, but not eating and sleeping too much were signs of deep depression. I'd decided to use anorexia as a way out of this world. That way, no one else could point the finger at Charlie as the reason for my suicide. A good friend got me out of that frame of mind, and I finally took a stand.

Casey, my friend from grade school, said to me, "My friend, you have been carrying on about leaving Charlie for quite some time now. Seeing the misery in your troubled life, how long is it going to be before you step up to the plate?" She said that she hoped I would take care of the problem before it destroyed both Charlie and me. She said the way I was going, it could take forever and wondered if my anguish was always going to be the center of my life.

Casey made me see what I needed to aim for. I needed to stop grumbling to my friends. Without realizing it, I must have been draining their spirits. Marley, another dear friend, and Casey gave me the strength to go forward with my life. I did not have to be an enabler for Charlie or the victim of a manipulative, controlling alcoholic.

I insisted on putting the house up for sale, and it sold in no time (before the sign was even in the ground). Charlie's parents did not know we had hired a real estate agent. They talked to me in the mall, and I told them to phone their son. They did not believe our circumstances could be so bad and wanted us to meet in their home to talk things out (especially about the letter).

It was already too late. At the meeting, they learned that Mulligan and I were moving to a two-bedroom apartment not far from his school. Charlie had moved closer to his work. I was hoping everything would be okay, but I was wrong.

My next door neighbor, who had become a real pal, came over to help me pack. We choked up from the turmoil; after all, it was my very first home with our little family. Charlie's drinking and gambling, however, had torn us apart, and that was not all. A divorce means that your friends leave you in the end too. How sad. I knew that Charlie liked his beer when we were dating, but I never saw the signs of alcoholism then. My home life had taught me that drinking was okay, as long as the drinkers did not abuse their spouses.

In the early years of our marriage, we couldn't afford to buy liquor. I wasn't working, so we had to use his pay to buy our groceries and pay for other needs. We couldn't afford extras. When I worked full time—and after we installed the pool—our troubles began.

I left to live in my apartment just around the corner, and Charlie moved out of the house. Mulligan was hardly at home because of school and activities with his friends. I do not think my son knew of the danger I was in at that time.

One evening, I came home from a twelve-hour shift to find Charlie sitting on the sofa. I asked him how he had gotten in; he said he had a key. I hadn't given him one, so the only other source would have been Mulligan.

The next day at work, Charlie's parents were outside in the mall waiting for me and pleaded with me to give Charlie a second chance. They assured me that he was going to quit drinking. My son also asked me to give his father another chance.

Charlie told Mulligan to call me one day at my work. He was supposed to tell me that his dad was going to commit suicide. I remembered, however, that a nurse I met once said that when someone announces he or she is going to commit suicide, it is just a threat. Think about it; anyone who is really going to kill him- or-herself does not typically let anyone else know. He or she may leave a note; otherwise, it is just another control maneuver.

In the fall, Charlie came by and asked me to go for a drive with him. We both loved Indian summer. The day was cloudless, and the sun was very warm. The air was rich with the scent of freshly fallen leaves. Thinking of going to the forest, I recalled fond memories from years past. Because of those rich memories, I let my guard down and agreed to go with him.

It was just a perfect day, a great day to get away from it all for a while. I was hoping things would go well for Mulligan's sake; I really wanted him to have a good relationship with Charlie.

Arriving at one of our favorite parks, we got out of the car and started to hike in. Walking deep into the forest, I noticed the colors of the leaves were as bright as any time I could remember. Going down a path, Charlie said, "This is it." I asked what he was talking about. He told me to wait there. I said no, but he kept walking back toward the parking lot. I followed him. He told me to stay still because he was getting a rope with which to hang himself. I told him he could do whatever he wanted, but I wasn't going to witness any of it. I called his bluff. He was the boy who cried wolf. People in a genuinely suicidal frame of mind would never reveal what they were about to do.

I had regular work-related stress, the stress of his parents, and the stress of dealing with Charlie. At that time, he was calling and then hanging up the phone after I would answer. There was no more fight left in me. I finally relented and told him he could move back, but for my safety's sake, if there were any signs of drinking (Charlie was a mean drunk), I would leave him for good.

A year went by, and I saw no signs of drinking. Dating Charlie became fun. I suggested we buy another house, hoping it might be the home we retired in. We decided to buy our second brand-new home; it was made to order, with custom colors and carpet, a special ceiling, and many other extras.

Our new residence was out in the country in what had been a farmer's field. In spite of planning and praying, my dream was shattered about two years later.

The house was not far from a stretch of very bad highway. In the winter, the roads became icy, and snowdrifts accumulated quickly. Many accidents occurred on that stretch of highway.

One February morning, I was running late for work and tried to take a short cut that led me up a hill and around a sharp bend in the road. I made it up the hill but noticed, going down, that I was on black ice. I prayed to my Father in heaven to help me. I knew not to slam on the brakes, so I gently pumped them and managed to miss all the posts, poles and curves. I came to a dead stop just before a steep snowdrift, but I was stuck.

Before long, two men came along on the flat stretch of road; when they saw me, they offered to push me out. They helped me get my car turned around and headed in the right direction. I hailed a police officer driving down the main drag. He was also on black ice and slid about a quarter of a mile before he was able to stop and turn around. I told him what happened and suggested that the dangerous section of road be blocked.

Just then, we spotted a car coming down the hill—a compact with two girls in it. They couldn't stop either and slid into my car. They would have hit me too if I hadn't jumped out of the way. Thankfully, there was not too much damage to my car. Then a stake-bed truck came sliding down the hill, heading straight for where we were congregated. I shouted to the police officer to run, and the truck came within inches of us before finally coming to a stop. This all took place within a span of fifteen minutes. In the end, my car was still drivable, but I was late for work. Later that evening, we hosted a murder mystery party. I could have been the corpse!

On another day, I was coming back from shopping when the car in front of me skidded. I tried to get out of the way, but my vehicle was on black ice too. Heading for a steep drop-off I called out to my heavenly Father to please help me stop. Two men going the other direction saw this, recognized me and the car (they knew Charlie), and turned around to help. They said they were in awe as they watched me stop just in time. I was on the very edge of a small cliff and about to go over, but the car miraculously came to a halt. An angel was beside me on the road that day.

Another time, my friends and I were out to dinner. The weather was changing fast, so before starting my drive home I went to my parents' house and called Charlie to find out how bad the weather was at home. He said it was fine and wondered why I asked. He told me to come on home. I thought I had beaten the storm, so I left my parents' place with confidence that driving would be okay.

However, about fifteen minutes into the ride home, the drifts became very bad, and the snow was blowing so hard that we were experiencing whiteouts. I couldn't see the road signs and I didn't know where I was on the highway. We hadn't lived in the area for long, and I was scared. Again, I cried out to my Father in heaven (in not so nice words) for help, when finally a brave man in a four wheeler passed me, taking the lead and then slowing so that I could follow. If it hadn't been for him, I think I would still be crawling down that highway with a convoy of cars behind me. My angel was beside me once again.

When I arrived home, our neighbor was out shoveling his driveway, and Charlie was shoveling ours. The neighbor asked why I would leave the city, knowing that the weather was so bad, instead of staying with my mom and dad. I answered, "Charlie told me it was fine out here." My neighbor turned to Charlie and if looks could kill, I am sure Charlie would be dead now.

Charlie began spending a lot of time at the neighbor's house and talking in their garage. I knew something was up and caught him drinking. Later, I figured out that Charlie had been hiding his beer in the trunk of the car. When I was at work, he got the beer out to drink with the neighbors. I had to keep my promise to myself that I would leave him.

We had a mutual friend who owned a restaurant outside of our town. She would order Charlie's beer and keep it in the restaurant's refrigerator. When I worked late hours, he went to her restaurant and picked it up. What a friend *she* was. She knew about Charlie's drinking problem. I suppose that she thought he had his own mind and should do what he liked. They were both drinkers and supported each other, even if it meant harming their own health.

Thinking back now, she had no idea about the harm Charlie could do, and had done to me after he went over his limit. But maybe she did, because drinkers love their own kind. Oh well, some friend!

She showed up once at our home very early in the morning. Her spouse had hit her badly. She asked Charlie if she could stay in her van, parked in our driveway, so that she could be away from her husband. Charlie said yes, but then he asked her to come inside. She declined the offer and slept in her van. I stayed in bed to avoid getting involved. Charlie never said a word to me, and I never mentioned it.

Charlie had spread stories that weren't true about me to our friends and neighbors. I hope I never find out what he said. Someone once said to me, "People who know you know you well. People who don't know you don't care, but all people like to listen to gossip."

Living in a small town and attending church services there, I sat in the congregation nearly every week. The church members noticed that Charlie was not attending. The women's group I joined knew me and saw me helping at events to raise money for the missions. Even the pastor saw this, but he still believed the rumors that Charlie was spreading about me. Such gossip was damaging to me. The hurt he personally caused me and his attempts to break my spirit were just too much.

The leader of the women's group believed everything Charlie said. She even spied on me for him. She reported what I was wearing and even gave him information about events happening in my life. She then proceeded to tell the pastor everything she'd discovered.

A friend of hers came to see me at work to tell me what she had heard; to this day, I wonder why no one could see through Charlie. In a time of need, I could certainly have used some support—not criticism.

Later, an invitation came to me. The ladies from the church heard that I was moving and wanted to throw me a going-away party. The problem with that was that I already knew too much, so I said thanks but no thanks.

At home things tensions were escalating. My mail was always opened, and Charlie always had an excuse for opening it. He started intercepting phone calls and messages. When I would ask, Charlie always said that no one had called. He began accusing me of having an affair. He asked, "Who are you expecting a call from, your boyfriend?" He began attempting to exert even more control over me. We had invested so much time in our relationship, but the way I was being treated was just overwhelming. I asked Charlie to give me a divorce, but his answer was always no.

I caught Charlie drinking when I came home early from work one day. Again, I asked him for a divorce, but he said he would not divorce me. He thought he could keep me as a prisoner in my own home. I was feeling like a lioness in a cage, kept locked up in my own environment.

At that time, I had a male friend who owned a yacht. We spent time walking and talking and enjoying some great moments together. Later, the relationship did develop into a short-lived affair, which I allowed to happen deliberately because I was so hurt and angry with Charlie. I thought my friend was a great person who was lonely in his marriage. I talked about and planned an escape on his yacht, but in the end, he was determined to stay in his marriage.

I must have been quite desperate at that time. I had no money to leave Charlie. I felt I was wrong and should repent for having been so desperate. Things were getting worse with Charlie, and I did have the odd affair to keep my sanity and feel appreciated.

When I caught him drinking, I reminded him about the promise I had made to myself. I was in a weakened emotional condition and feeling very unloved when this second affair happened. I was already being accused anyway, so I reasoned why not? Then I escorted Charlie to the other bedroom and told him that he could have his own life back. At that moment, I considered myself a single woman, but I still felt there was no way out. I did what I had to do; however, two wrongs never make a right.

I was looking for evidence one day to see how I could get out of the marriage. I went searching in Charlie's drawer. At the very back, hidden under some clothes, I found a yellow receipt folded up. How brilliant! Charlie was thinking I would never find that piece of evidence. I questioned him about the meaning of the receipt, but he had nothing to say.

Before work the next day, I went to see a friend to ask if she knew what the receipt was about. Her life was so unlike my sheltered world that I figured she would know. She told me it looked like Charlie had been to a loan shark for money, offering our household goods as collateral. She told me to be very careful. If it was true, such a bad guy might either come after all our possessions or harm Charlie and even me if the loan wasn't paid as agreed. Then she asked me about the pills Charlie was taking because she'd witnessed him taking some. I knew nothing about it. All this time, I thought his drinking was bad enough—now drugs. What next?

Arriving home the very next night, I was afraid to go into the house. My hand was on the doorknob, but suddenly I felt apprehensive about going ahead. My intuition told me that something was wrong, but I couldn't identify what. I immediately moved away from the door but then ignored my intuition, saying to myself: *What are you doing? You're just being paranoid!* I then proceeded to enter the house.

Charlie had set the table with a burning scented candle, and everything was perfect—almost like a fine dining room at a resort. This display was in the entertaining room of our unloving home. The meal was cooked to perfection and presented well. The whole dinner must have taken a lot of time and thought because it was delicious.

My warning lights began flashing after we finished eating. The two of us were having a deep conversation, and then Charlie suddenly seemed out of sorts. Having worked a long day, I left the room. I came out of the shower, wearing my housecoat. Then Charlie stormed into the room, forced me on the bed, and grabbed my throat with his bare hands, yelling and shaking me very hard. I was in shock and was so exhausted and frightened that I wasn't able to focus on his words. He told me to keep out of his personal business. Then he said, "I will show you the meaning of the paper you found."

Thinking my life was about to end, I cried out to my Father in heaven. I could see the evil in Charlie, and I asked the Lord to please take me home then because I was no longer able to take such abuse.

An angel must have come to my rescue because Charlie was forced to back away; it was like an invisible hand pushing him away from me. By then, I was seeing stars and blacking out when Charlie left the room. Eventually, he passed out in the spare room.

Later, I yelled that I would be gone by morning. But saying that was a mistake—especially to someone with booze and possibly drugs in him. It's best sometimes to leave your plans a secret. I would have been safer had I left quietly.

I knew the loan sharks would take the contents of the house. Without hesitation, I obeyed my promise to myself and to my Father in heaven and left early the next morning.

Because Charlie had proven irresponsible with financial matters in the past, I paid the mortgage every month. Charlie was supposed to pay the other bills such as taxes. However, he hadn't paid the taxes for the two years we lived there. Without a doubt, Charlie knew that the city would have taken our home within the third year of no payment.

Each time I asked him if the taxes had been paid, he showed me a bill that said *paid* in big bold letters. I should have checked the date. The taxes and the date last paid were written on the receipt in very small print. Charlie led me to believe the taxes had been paid by yelling at me and showing me the receipt. By the time I found out the truth, we were two years in arrears. He stayed in the house for some time after I stopped making payments.

I knew I had to get away from Charlie. It was six o'clock in the morning, and he had just left for work. Once again, I made a mistake; I told him I would be gone when he arrived home that night. Two hours after I left, he apparently came home and changed the locks on all the doors. I had forgotten some important papers, but when I went back for them, I couldn't get in. Even though I was paying the mortgage, I could not legally enter. I could be charged with breaking and entering.

Later, I ran into a detective I had known for many years. He suggested that I have a police escort accompany me—two policemen from his place of work. They did their job but failed to help me retrieve a painting that my mother had done. I asked the officers to please let me get my belongings, but I was told I had to go to court for the artwork. By that time, my son came to the rescue and asked to get the picture for me. Charlie said, however, that the art was his and that my mother had painted it for him.

Charlie had his usual grin on his face when he said it. Looking back over the years, I realized that facial expression meant he was not telling the truth. (A recent program on television cautioned people to look for devious facial signals. Charlie's was a real smirk.)

At that time, I began to break down emotionally. Charlie was threatening me, but an angel was with me. Mulligan backed Charlie into a corner and told me to get my things. He warned his father not to stop me.

I pray God's wisdom will inspire anyone wanting to leave a controlling and obsessive person to prearrange the taking of all important papers and belongings before announcing any plans to do so. It's best to say nothing to anyone before hiring a truck. My advice is to leave town or go to a safe place fast, and stay safe. Many resources are available, but quietly begin preparations before it is too late. Always know your options.

Chapter 6

Real Trouble

Over time, I had become friends with the nurse at my doctor's office. When I told her I wanted to keep my problems away from my family, she suggested I stay with her for a few weeks. Since my furniture was at the house with Charlie—and he had changed the locks—I had no possessions to speak of. I accepted her wonderful offer, bringing only the clothes I needed and leaving the rest at my parents' house.

One day, a client I had known for several years came in the shop. When his cut and style were finished, he asked me to tea. This client noticed that I was not my usual bubbly self, and his observation was correct. I was feeling down, so I went to tea with him when my shift was over. I told him everything that had been happening the last few years; then he told me he was in the same situation with his wife and that I was welcome to have a room at his lake house. His place was big enough to accommodate me.

I took him up on his generosity, paid board, and placed myself in a small room. He said his wife had kicked him out of the family home after a fight, during which she had hit him on the head with a sharp object. I asked him why he hadn't called the police. He said he didn't want to admit he was the victim in an abusive relationship. From my volunteer work in an abuse center, I learned there are just as many men as there are women being abused. But most men don't want to admit to it, fearing they will be perceived as weak and unmanly.

I went to his house on the water, and we enjoyed each other's company. As our friendship grew, he suggested that I begin divorce proceedings if it was what I really wanted. I started asking around for an attorney to hire. I made a choice, and it turned into a nightmare. The lawyer gave me a price, and I thought we had come to an agreement. I was to pay him a retainer (a lot for those days) and give him half immediately (as the retainer), which he said would take us through processing the separation papers. I was to pay the rest when the divorce papers came through.

However, the separation agreement was never generated, let alone processed. The attorney then sent me a huge bill for more than the original amount. I went to his office and told him he would get no more money from me. By that time, he had received more than $ 2,000, but I had nothing to show for it.

At the outset, I made it clear: all I wanted was out of the marriage, but the lawyer insisted that I get what I was owed. He told me I had rights because I'd been married to Charlie for twenty-three years. This lawyer was using the point system, which led me to believe the quoted price was in dollars—not in points. Therefore, the amount added up quickly. I was deceived by his dishonesty and had nothing to show for what I paid him.

It's too bad that Charlie did not simply agree to the divorce in the first place. Had he done so, we would not have had to go through the control game he was playing. It would not have been so costly for both of us and would have been much less of a strain on our mental and physical health.

One evening at the lake house, it had snowed so much that the city was shut down. People were asked to stay off the roads except for emergencies. I opened the door to go out, and all I saw was snow up past the door frame about eight feet deep. We had to shovel our way out from the inside. Plus, we had to wait for the snowplow to clear our driveway so we could get to the main road. This process took two days.

Having my own room at the lake house, I wanted to pay rent, but my friend refused because he really liked having the company. He was many years older than I and was a kind, safe person to be with. He treated me and my friends as sweetly as any gentleman possibly could. He could never do enough for my friend Marley and me. Even though he did not expect it, I paid him rent. He saved every penny that I had paid him and gave it back to me when I decided to move forward with my new life. To this day, I thank God that this friend crossed my path at just the right time.

He and I went together to find a new place for me to live because our living arrangement was causing problems with our estranged spouses. We feared something bad would happen to us, because they were individually making it clear that they were unhappy, and jealous of our friendship. I finally found a place, moved in, and got settled. Or so I thought.

One night in March, after having worked a twelve-hour day, Charlie came calling. I wasn't thinking when the buzzer went off. I thought it was my friend from the cottage and went downstairs to open the outside door slightly. I wanted to hear what he had to say. When I realized that it was Charlie I told him that I needed to turn off my shower and would be back down in a minute.

Before I realized it, Charlie had his foot in the door and had forced his way inside. I ran upstairs to shut my apartment door and turn the shower off, but Charlie was right behind me. He forced me through the door and past the living room into the bedroom. With only my bathrobe on, I was particularly vulnerable, and he slammed me onto the bed. I screamed for help, but no one came to my rescue. In hindsight, I should have yelled *fire!* Perhaps then someone would have heard me and come to help.

By that time, Charlie was forcing himself on me. At the same time, he was tying my robe belt around my neck. The next thing I remember was Charlie being pulled away from me. Since no one was there, my protector had to be my guardian angel again because I was slipping into darkness.

Then I realized I had caught a break. I saw my chance and to the best of my ability ran for help. I was able to find the landlord's mother. She and I went back to see if Charlie was still there. Thank God, he wasn't. Then I called a friend who told me to call the police, but I hesitated because I couldn't do that to our son's father. Then I called my girlfriend but got no answer and had to leave a message telling her what had happened.

Just then, I heard heavy, loud footsteps coming up the stairs. Thinking it was Charlie, I was stricken with fear. I told my friend on the phone that I didn't know what I would do if he kicked the door in because I had no other way to get out of the apartment. My friend told me to put the phone down and yell through the door to see who was there. Carefully checking with the chain on, I saw that it was the police. They had come to see if I was okay. The police told me Charlie was at the police station and confessed what he had done. Looking back on it, I believe that he just wanted to look good.

Around this time, the girlfriend I called had retrieved my message and came over to check on me. The police advised me to have Charlie arrested on forced rape charges, but I again hesitated because he was Mulligan's father. My friend and the police officers asked, "If Charlie had hurt someone else, would that have been okay?" I agreed to take their advice, hoping it might stop Charlie's rage from harming someone else in the future.

To my surprise, I wasn't allowed to clean myself up or even put clothes on. I had to wear only my bathrobe, my winter coat, and my high boots. I had to sit in the front seat of the police car while the officer drove me to the hospital. What a sight I must have been.

The hospital had called a person from the Center for Women in Trauma to see me. Lo and behold, it was a lady who had been in to get her hair done earlier that morning. She had handed me her card while at the shop and told me to call if I ever needed help. She came highly recommended by the service and support organization helping women.

I had to go through the whole rape kit, which takes a couple of hours. It is a very invasive process and was quite an ordeal. I'm certain anyone who has been raped would agree. I was then told they would have to keep my bathrobe, the only piece of clothing I had with me and I had an emotional meltdown. The staff showed me compassion. Since it was my husband who had raped me, they allowed me to keep and wear my only robe. Charlie was going to have to face charges. I arrived back at my apartment around four o'clock in the morning and still showed up for work at 9:30 a.m. the next day.

One of my former neighbors called me at work. She asked me why I was working after the night I'd had. Believing that the previous night's events were being kept under wraps, I asked her why she asked the question. Well, I found out! The incident was already on the news and would be in the newspaper—without our names. She had been clued in by the address given. Before leaving our last home, I told this same neighbor why I was leaving. I really don't think she believed me at first because everyone in that small town thought Charlie was a real gentleman. I thanked her for the call.

I then had to call my parents to let them know the truth. Except for a few marks on my neck I was okay. I told my boss and everyone at work about the incident. Thankfully, our names weren't mentioned on the news or in the newspaper; only our addresses were identified. Because of the way I had hidden my troubles from everyone, this turmoil was hard for many to believe. Now everything was revealed.

Working in the mall was a blessing because it had security guards twenty-four hours a day. Charlie had begun stalking me. Initially, it seemed harmless, but I soon learned that stalking is not a sign of a healthy mind. I had to be very careful from then on. Charlie would send flowers to me at work or leave a rose on the driver's side of my car. Flowers seemed nice but scary at the same time. Obviously, he still had a key to my car. In addition to flowers, he left notes and stalked me on the nights I worked late. I should have changed my car locks, but it was the last thing on my mind just then.

By that time, there was a restraining order against Charlie, but he ignored the order. I guess he wanted to exert his control over me. From then on, I had to get the security guards to walk me to my car on the nights I worked twelve-hour shifts. I feared for my life, and now I know that restraining order situations can be very dangerous. The police can't be monitoring someone all hours of the day. In retrospect, I should have moved away quickly and secretly.

One evening, my male friend and I went out to celebrate my birthday with a nice dinner. It was late spring. The restaurant was out in the country by a lake. Years ago, it had been a busy lodge. I had a habit of checking all parking lots for Charlie, but I hadn't thought to do so this time. What a mistake! After dinner, we were leaving to go back to my friend's place when I noticed bright lights heading my way. I had trained my eyes to always look down from the ground and then up, which helped me see if it was Charlie. I noticed the special license plate that I had given him as a gift a few years earlier and saw him in the driver's seat. Charlie waited for me to leave first because, as you will see, he had no intention of moving his car until I did.

Exiting the lodge, I was approaching a stop sign when Charlie rammed my car from behind. I then drove forward slowly, with my hand on the horn, so that people could see my friend and I were in trouble; Charlie was right up my bumper. He continued banging into my car all the way down the exit road, no doubt hoping I would lose control. We were on a dirt road, heading toward the paved main highway.

It was a beautiful evening, just before dusk. Children were out with their parents and people were walking their dogs. Because there were no sidewalks so far out in the country, people were talking to their neighbors on the side of the road, witnessing this spectacle play-out.

Charlie's anger was out of control. As I approached the highway, another car pulled out in front of me hemming me in. Charlie must have hired a friend to block me. He thus had time to ram his car into mine at will. Who knows what might have happened to my dear friend and me? We could've been severely injured or even killed.

Fortunately I saw an opening and was able to cut around the blocking car. Charlie's friend didn't notice a tiny space between his car and a stop sign. Thanks to my car being small, I quickly squeezed by him and saw that the main road was clear of traffic.

There was a provincial police office about a quarter of a mile away, and I drove directly there. I pulled in, and standing there was the secretary of the police force calling us to get inside quickly. She said she had heard my horn all the way down from the corner and wondered what was happening. To her amazement, she saw Charlie pushing my car into oncoming traffic and the other car trying to block me from getting out of Charlie's way. Now I had at least one reliable witness to help me with Charlie.

The secretary told us the reason she was at the office was that she thought she had left the coffee pot on. Charlie was so angry with me for being out with my friend at this particular diner that he hadn't noticed he was in front of the provincial police office. The building was small and sat back off the main highway.

As I was getting out of my car, I was afraid he was going to ram into me again. He suddenly realized where he was and took off. Charlie had been issued a restraining order to stay away from me, and he had clearly violated that order.

With this incident, the provincial police (as well as the city police) became involved. The secretary at the provincial police office ordered the officers on duty to get to the office fast. When they arrived, lo and behold, they were the same two officers who had come to my house the evening I went to retrieve my personal belongings (the night I was not able to get my picture).

When they realized who I was, they apologized. At the time of that incident, I think the police thought it was only a "woman's thing," and it was just someone complaining about her husband. They treated that past incident as a simple domestic quarrel. Back then, the police were not trained to recognize the potential dangers involved in a domestic call. Now, when a domestic call comes in, the officials at headquarters send more than one officer, and they make sure the officers are well protected against potential violence.

Later that night, the local city police went to pick up Charlie at his parent's home in order to take him to jail. He had committed a serious crime—dangerous driving—and he had been caught. But when the city police officers arrived at his dad's home without a search warrant, they could not enter the residence.

Charlie's father sent the officers away, saying that Charlie was in bed. It was then eleven o'clock at night, and by the terms of the restraining order that was Charlie's curfew time.

The next morning, the police arrived at Charlie's work place. (By now Charlie's dad had retired.) It was there that the police put Charlie in handcuffs to take him to jail.

Everyone who knew Charlie and his dad also knew the family's dirty little secret about Charlie's drinking. His drinking habit got him into trouble because it derailed an otherwise sound mind.

I'd always warned Mulligan to keep our name out of the paper and not bring grief to the family. I was ashamed that his dad would be the cause of such public humiliation and grief. Even though Mulligan was twenty years old, I hadn't told him anything about what was going on after I left his dad.

As if that weren't enough at the time, I was being harassed at work by a girl who wanted me fired because I was one of the most requested stylists in the shop. She was going about it sneakily, telling the staff and the bosses, falsehoods about my character. She told many vicious lies about my professional disposition.

The day I was to be let go, my boss came to me and said, "We have just fired that girl." A friend of hers— one of the staff members—had gone behind the girl's back and informed the boss that the girl was planning to leave to open her own shop. She intended to do so in two weeks, which just happened to be one of the busiest times of the year.

The reason she wanted me fired was that she could then easily hire me. I guess she was thinking that the stress would affect me so badly that she could allay my worries by offering me a position and obtain my well-established client base. Thanks to my Father in heaven, I was not let go from my job. I am also thankful for the discernment to know what this devious employee was really like.

I then asked myself why the bosses listened to this fairly new staff person; she had worked there only a year compared to my five years' experience with them. They knew my working habits, my productivity and client base, and I was concerned about their loyalty. The truth was revealed in the end, and I continued working there happily.

Another time at work, a lady came to get a perm. I suggested she should upgrade from the perm she wanted because the less expensive perm would not do well on her color-treated hair. She told me the more expensive perm would take all the money she had with her that day, but she agreed to buy the better product.

When the perm was almost done, she suddenly became very ill. Taking the perm rods out and gently pouring warm water over her hair, I started drying her hair quickly. Then I went to call her a cab. I asked her to please go to the hospital. However, there was a problem. I only had five dollars on me, and she had no money after paying her bill. I told this to the cab driver, and he said that the five dollars was enough because the hospital was only minutes away.

I had given him my last penny, but by the end of that day my tips had been really good—especially for our slow time of year. We had not been very busy that month, and my rent was due. Interestingly, I made enough money in tips to pay the mortgage. A few months later, that same lady came back with the five dollars I had given the cab driver. I truly did not expect her to do that (more angels by my side.)

On another occasion at work, a friend came in; she was crying and told me that her job was ending in two weeks. About five hours later, another client came in, exhibiting a joy that was enough to make me curious. I asked her, "Why are you so joyous on this fine day?" She told me that she had just retired from her job at the same place where my friend worked (the one who was losing her job). I asked her if she knew my friend, and she did. I told her the story and suggested that she refer my friend to her boss for an interview.

About a month later, my friend came in with a spring in her step and a smile from ear to ear; she told me she had a job. I discovered that it was the same job my other client had quit. To this day, she doesn't have a clue about what took place that day. Obviously another angel had been at work, and even though I had stress in my home life, there were still good things happening around me.

After my estranged husband faced charges of rape, dangerous driving, and an attempt to cause bodily harm with a motor vehicle, the police suggested I leave town. I asked why I should leave; my security was my job, my family, and my friends. And this was the town where I grew up. They responded that even with a restraining order, they couldn't be with me night and day.

That same night, I was driving with my friend Marley when a rock hit my car. I looked to see who had thrown the rock but saw no one. At the time, I thought nothing of it. But knowing something like that could be a potential danger in the future, I kept my guard up.

The following week, I was getting my car filled with gas when the young attendant asked me if I knew that my car tires were very low. My wheels were almost touching the ground. I said that because it was a sports car, it was supposed to have low-profile tires. She then replied, "No, I mean the air is low." She told me that she would fill the tires if I had time to wait. I told her I would make time for her to adjust them.

The following day at work, I was talking to a race car driver who had previously been in the shop for a haircut. I told him about the recent tire situation. The gentleman asked me if I liked to drive my sports car fast around corners, and I nodded. He said somebody else probably knew that because of the way all the tires were deflated. I could have tipped or rolled the car, especially while driving fast around corners. Another angel seemed to be watching over me.

Chapter 7

The Long Journey

TAKING THE ADVICE OF THE police and considering the recent events with my car, I went to my boss and gave him my two-week notice. I left town in my car with only my personal belongings.

When I left Charlie, I walked away from the house, leaving all the antiques I had paid for, gifts from my friends, and everything else. He never paid the mortgage after I stopped paying it. I kept hoping he would want to straighten up his life, admit he had a problem, and stop his drinking. I even hoped his family would help him; as a matter of fact, his dad did help him a little.

Charlie's father knew the police chief. The family was counseled to send Charlie to a hospital out of town for evaluation. This action would allow him to avoid being sent to prison where he wouldn't be so proud of his behavior toward his wife. Inmates frown on men who abuse women. Charlie would have experienced a horrific fate; he may not even have lived to tell the tale.

The time came to say my good-byes to everyone. First, I went to my son, now twenty-one years old and becoming a good man. I had confidence that I could cut the apron strings, and he would be okay. Then I went to say goodbye to my parents and my friends—that was the hardest thing to do. No one knew how long I would have to stay away from my family, and the police advised me to tell no one where I was going.

With tears in my eyes, I started on my new adventure. It was a bittersweet departure. My mom's cousin and her family were heading west in the direction I was going. They invited me to follow them so that we could watch over each other on the trip. That was a welcome gesture, as it had taken me five hours to arrive at their place. A rest was indeed called for.

The next day, we started out after breakfast and traveled across the Ambassador Bridge, driving up through the United States side. We traveled thirteen hours, and we were all exhausted when we finally stopped. After supper, we got rooms at a lodge and went to bed. The next day, we made it to Duluth, Minnesota, where we made time to do some shopping. Shortly thereafter, we went to a hotel and crashed.

We got up really early the next day so that we could meet our next goal, getting to where my two sisters lived. We were hoping to arrive at our destination around three o'clock that same day.

I arrived at my sister's place and stayed for a week. It was special because I would be there for the birthday of both of my sisters; they had been born on the same day but a year apart. They were encouraging me to stay and find work there so that we could all be together. The only problem was that I had made a promise to the friend who had helped me get away from Charlie, and who had assisted me financially. He had arranged for me to stay with his sister on the west coast until I could get my feet on the ground and find work. I truly wish I had listened to my sisters because the west coast arrangement turned into a situation from hell.

For my big send-off my sisters, aunt, and cousins all met for breakfast. I had many miles to go before reaching my ultimate destination, and this time I would be driving alone. After the long and tearful good-byes, I went on my way.

I traveled past Banff and Jasper. For someone who had never driven outside of Ontario, I was in total awe at the sight of my maker's creation. The Rocky Mountains are worth anyone's investment in time. I had to take a deep breath, trying to inhale the beauty around me. I have never forgotten that majestic view.

Even on a sunny day in August, there was a little bit of fresh snow on the peaks of those mountains. Over the horizon in front of me was the brightest blue sky; it reminded me of the western movie Big Sky Montana.

The first stop in my journey across the mountains of western Canada was Revelstoke. What a place! Right in the middle of those beautiful surroundings was an information center with huge, wide windows, where I stayed a while to get some rest and to take in the view.

Then I started traveling up the mountain again. I turned up the volume of the radio, and began to speed. After all, I was on my way to freedom in the middle of God's country. Because it was Sunday, there was hardly any traffic. Speeding along with the radio on and windows down, my blond hair blowing in the wind, I faintly heard a message in my ear saying, "Slow down." I looked up at that endless blue sky and said to myself: *Heck no.* I proceeded to speed up even more and turned up the music even louder. The voice said again and louder: "Slow down." Again, I said to myself: *This is too much fun, being free on this particularly wide highway, almost free from traffic, with the music playing and the gorgeous vista all around.*

I put the pedal to the metal, and turned my radio up to the max. "Slow down!" The voice in my mind got my attention this time. Looking to my left, I saw a sheer drop-off. Not far off the road to the right was a massive wall of granite. Taking in the beautiful but dangerous surroundings finally got me to listen to my heavenly Father's voice, and I paid attention.

I remembered seeing the movie, "The Other Side of the Mountain." It was about an Olympic skier who'd found herself going fast down a mountain just before an accident that left her in a wheelchair. If my brakes were to fail, no one would recognize me or my car. Because of the curving highway, the potential plunge down the side, and the nearly three-quarters-full gas tank, the car would definitely have blown up. I moved to a slower lane and continued at a more reasonable pace. With the radio turned down and my prayers said, I continued on my journey.

Feeling confident, I felt the drive become routine, and I began to let my mind wander to a time when I was around fourteen years old. My mom asked if I would like to volunteer at one of the hospitals. I said yes, and I was soon off to my first day of training. The hospital staff gave me a crisp candy-striped cap and apron with the biggest bow I had ever seen. The uniform itself made all the young volunteers feel important and special.

Walking down the main halls with the nurses and doctors up ahead, we thought we were almost like them. We were taken to a training room, and our instructor suggested that we get a bed pan from a closet. When we were told what to do, I couldn't hand in the uniform fast enough; I left and never looked back. The sight of a dirty diaper made me gag when I babysat my own sisters, or my neighbor's children. I couldn't picture myself cleaning up after an adult or any other kinds of messes I might encounter in a hospital. Looking back, I sure was a delicate little thing.

My mind traveled to when I was in the hospital giving birth to Mulligan. My nurse was a nun. The way she flew in and out of the room, I decided to call her "the flying nun." Another nurse from the pediatric ward saw me leaving my room to go see Mulligan. She told me to get back to my room because she thought I was in her ward. I was that small. Oh how I wish I could describe the look on her face when I told her that I had just had a baby and was going to have a peek at him.

I think we were tough on the flying nun, since some of the ladies had many children to my one. None of the new moms in my ward was in a quiet mood, especially on New Year's Eve night. A gathering formed in my room. But since we only had water and pills to celebrate with, the celebration was less than fun. Before I took my pills, I asked the flying nun what each one was for. I told her I didn't believe in taking pills unless absolutely necessary. She insisted that the medication was what the doctor ordered and for me to take them all. Then I proceeded to ask what each one did. As she was explaining, I responded, "I don't need this one or that one."

She said she wasn't going to leave the room until I had taken all of them. After she left, the party resumed, and jokes went around. We laughed and laughed. It wasn't long before the flying nun came to tell us off. She said it was now eleven o'clock, and we needed to quiet down. She turned the lights out; by then the pill began to take effect.

At two o'clock in the morning, my throat was feeling a little funny. One of the moms in our ward rang for help. When the nurse came to see what was wrong, she only had a mini flashlight with her. She told me that she saw nothing wrong and to go back to sleep. By four o'clock in the morning, I had to put my fingers down my throat so that I could swallow. The lady in the end bed heard the noise I was making. She called out each of our names, asking one by one if we were okay. When she said my name, all I could muster was "ugh."

In no time, I had nurses and two doctors coming and going because I was having a serious allergic reaction to the medication I'd taken. When they finally had my reaction under control, they asked my roommates not to wake me. I didn't wake up until eleven o'clock in the morning, and all the ladies in my ward said, "Good morning, Sleeping Beauty; what a night you had!" My only reply was, "See, I told that flying nun I knew there would be a problem, but she wouldn't listen."

Driving along the highway, I recalled a time when we took Mulligan to see Niagara Falls. I think he was four years old at the time. Marineland was just starting to become a popular attraction, so we made plans to go there. We decided to sit in the front row to see the dolphin show. Following the dolphins, out came the bigger sea mammals to do their tricks. One of them, followed by a second, leaped high in the air and landed back in the water with terrific force. We were thoroughly and completely soaked. We figured out why there were so many unclaimed seats in the front row, but all in all we had great fun.

Next, I remembered a tragic event that occurred one winter when I was a teen. The roads were very icy. A school bus driver's route crossed a railway track at the bottom of a valley. He was not particularly concerned about crossing the tracks because in all his years of experience, there had never been a train at the crossing. When he stopped at the bottom of the decline on this day, as usual, he saw no danger. But when he began to cross the tracks one of the children screamed that a train was coming. The children were having so much fun on their trip to school, and were making so much noise, that the driver didn't hear the warning.

Recognizing how much danger they were in, one of the children opened the back door of the school bus and jumped out. He was the only one to have done so. Unaware of what was about to occur, the rest remained in place. One of the students was a friend of mine. Though many were injured, she and a younger girl sitting beside her both died from internal injuries. The train hit squarely in the middle of the school bus where they were seated. I went to the funeral home to see my friend's family, and the other little girl's father asked me to come and see his daughter. I've never forgotten the trauma of those days.

I was saddened for my friend who would not finish high school and grow up. I had enrolled in the same school she attended and was scheduled to start the following year, hoping that we would become even deeper friends.

Another flashback of a lasting memory was when Charlie and I hosted a murder mystery party. We lived in the country in a small town with a population of about a thousand people. Our story was to take place at a resort, with a bunch of students who were attending a reunion. Across from the resort there was a stand of pine trees beside a creek, an arched bridge crossed over the creek and went to their lodging. It was the perfect description because our friend owned a diner in the country with a room that had a view along a creek. She had given us permission to have the party there. Other than the arched bridge, it couldn't have been closer to the scene of the mystery.

While I was at her place discussing the murder scene, a man got up from his table and asked us who had been murdered, when, and why hadn't it been on the news. We laughed and told him that we were planning a murder mystery party. We had invited two tables of friends for the party. When Charlie went to get the groceries for the big event, one of the people in front of him remarked that he must be the one hosting the mystery game. Small towns know everything.

On another occasion, Charlie was asked to look after our friend's home and restaurant. They were a great couple who had created a cozy and welcoming dining environment downstairs. The upstairs had been turned into a nice two-bedroom apartment. They were smart people who would close the restaurant and head south every year around New Year's.

A friend had been staying with them and volunteered to look after their place through the harsh winter months until they returned. This arrangement was agreed upon, and our friends departed happy, knowing that their business and home would be well looked after. Because of the unforeseen weather their friend had to abandon the plan because his own home had developed problems. Severe ice storms, heavy snows and extremely low temperatures caused his own power to be cut off, causing the old-fashioned radiators in his home to freeze up. When he departed, he let us know he wouldn't be able to return for two months, and the owners would be away until spring. He asked us to please look after the place for him.

Over the next few weeks, all went well at the restaurant until one morning when Charlie found the power had been compromised. The property had lost its electricity. We would learn later that animals had torn away some of the outside insulation wrapped around a fuse box leading into the house. Following an ice storm and extremely cold weather, ice had formed inside the fuse box and it had frozen.

The owners had a fish tank with an Oscar, a type of fish that was the owner's favorite pet. When you tapped on the glass, the fish would come and get rubbed by the friction on the glass, which he loved. Oscar always slept on the left side of the fish tank.

With the power out, we called the owners to tell them what had happened. I asked them about Oscar and whether or not they wanted me to put a blanket around the tank to try and keep the fish from freezing. (She said the tank had a heater in it but to please keep an eye on Oscar.) I told her he was fine so far because his mouth looked like he was kissing the side of his tank. (Oscar fish make a kissing motion when they eat the algae along the sides of the tank.)

Shortly after our call to the owners, the people from the insurance company came by. When we went inside, we discovered Oscar was dead.

Concurrently, having remedied his own problems with his home, the gentleman who was originally watching the property returned, just in time for this disaster. After considerable discussion, we took Oscar and threw him in a snow bank. Later, we all realized that the spring thaw would reveal our folly, so we decided to put Oscar in the creek. Now, trying to find something as small as a frozen Oscar in deep snow is not easy, but we accomplished the task. Taking his frozen carcass to the nearby creek, we deposited him there.

The owner's wife called one evening, and we explained the calamity to her. She suggested we buy a new Oscar because she didn't want to have to tell her husband about the demise of his favorite pet.

Imagine all of us looking for this dead oval fish in a frozen creek. But as luck would have it, we found him still lying frozen on the surface. After taking some rough measurements of Oscar, our friend went to several pet shops to find a replacement about the right size. He couldn't find one in any of the nearby stores, so he had to drive about sixty miles into the city. He finally found a suitable one, but this Oscar was white. All was not lost, the lady at the store explained that about two hours after the fish is introduced into a fish tank, it would turn the dark color of the original Oscar. We placed the new and improved Oscar into the tank, and sometime later the owners walked in … early! We were all very much surprised by their coming back so soon.

After hearing about the storm, the owners were worried and wanted to come back in case anything needed to be done. They assured us that they could take care of everything from here on, so we wouldn't have to be responsible any longer.

Having spent hours on the road and having been gone for so long, the owner was feeling lonely for his pal. He went over to see Oscar, who had just turned from white to the darker color—just as the store lady said he would. I had been sweating buckets, not knowing how this new Oscar would react to the owner tapping on the glass. When the new Oscar felt the tapping on the tank, he went right for it. We all breathed a sigh of relief. The only difference with "new Oscar" was that this one liked to sleep on the other side of the tank. The owner thought the difference was because Oscar had missed him so much. To this day, I don't think the owner knows what really happened just hours before his arrival.

When we went to dinner with our neighbors the next night, we told them the story of what happened to our friend's pet. They suggested we could have had "old Oscar" freeze-dried, made into a door stop or a fish on a stick or even a statue. Poor Oscar was becoming the butt of everyone's joke. Thinking back now, I wonder what might have happened if the owner ever found out the truth about his real pet, especially if we hadn't found another Oscar.

About this time, I was approaching a lookout on the highway and decided to pull off to enjoy the majestic view. Oh what a sight! I then turned to go on my way when an old pickup truck, filled with furniture, passed me. My thought was that they were moving. I soon caught up to them, and as I studied their vehicle I saw that the poor wife was sleeping from boredom while I, in my little sports car, was far from being bored. Now it was time to have some fun.

I needed gas, so I pulled off at a service station. This gave the pickup truck driver plenty of time to get some distance from me. After filling up and getting back on the road, I eventually caught up to him. Now it was his turn to pull off the highway, so I thought that he was gone. But it wasn't for long; looking to my side, there he was. We were playing a game of cat and mouse. We kept this up for quite a distance, but eventually we came to a tollgate. After going through it, he went one way and I another.

Boredom was setting in again, and I slipped easily back into my reverie. I recalled a time when Mom and Dad gathered us up and went for a ride that eventually took us across a floating bridge. I remember that it was early spring—thawing time for us northerners—so the water level was higher than usual. On this particular day, the water was coming up to the car's undercarriage. Mom was afraid and kept saying, "We have to get off this bridge or we might go into the lake."

My dad, being brave or just plain stupid, continued along with the rest of the drivers, and all was well. I should mention that many others traveled across the floating bridge that day.

Another recollection took place in the winter, when the town had horse-drawn snow plows. A man led the horses, showing them the way, so that all the sidewalks were plowed. After repeating this process almost daily throughout the winter, I bet those horses knew their way. That era also had milk trucks that regularly delivered milk, bread, and sweets to homes once or twice a week.

I thought about the recent visit with my sisters. On one of our excursions we traveled up the mountain on a cable car and then hiked even higher on foot. We sat right on a mountain's edge, among mountain goats, and we fed them cheese. Coming back down, I remember feeling like I could see forever. When we had returned to the lower levels a moose with her young calf appeared on the path. We stopped and watched until they disappeared into the marsh. We didn't stay long, really, but what a sight! I haven't seen a moose that close since.

I was thinking again, this time about an incident that happened while Charlie and I were living in our second home (out in the country.) I was coming home from the city; as I came around the bend, several police vans were parked in front of a neighbor's house. The officers were putting two handcuffed women into one of the police cars. The other vehicles contained items the girls had stolen.

Another interesting but odd event took place one day while Charlie was watching football. I went to see my girlfriend down the street. She asked me to stay and have an iced tea with her out on her new patio. The day was unusually hot for late fall. My friend came outside with the drinks. She was passing one over to me when, from around the corner next door, several policemen came with their bulletproof vests on. They were armed and ready for action, their rifles pointing at doors, windows, and the street.

The man who was the head of the targeted household must have been involved with drugs or something of that nature to have been the object of such police action. It was a total surprise. We asked if we should leave the premises. Their reply was yes, since the owner of that house could be armed. We did leave and went across the street to watch all the action from inside our neighbor's home. Two hours later, the man in question hadn't surfaced. The officers left without him.

A memory about a time on the job came to mind. I had just been hired by a friend of my family. During the peak season, the business needed someone to work until the slower season came. The boss had invited me to their Christmas party, which was scheduled to take place in a few days. They told me that I could add to the savings jar, positioned near the door outside. All the money collected was to be used to help fund the upcoming outing.

One girl knew that I had to buy the equipment, rollers, picks, combs, brushes, and literally everything I needed to work a station in a hair salon. One day, she ran out of her rollers and asked to borrow mine. I wasn't using them at the time, so I graciously gave her my brand new rollers to use. When she returned the rollers, she gave me her old used ones.

I went to the boss and explained the situation. I even showed her the obviously aged rollers. Although she knew mine were new, she took the other girl's side because she was a long-time family friend. The experience taught me to watch out for myself because no one else was going to.

Christmas was fast approaching, and the party was in two days. I was working late that night and "little miss prissy" (the same girl who used my new rollers) saw an opportunity to frame me. I was standing outside, waiting for Charlie to pick me up. The evening was very cold, with a clear sky and a full moon. My nemesis said that I should come back inside. No one expected me to wait out in the cold, so I went inside. She told me to wait there for him and that she would be right back. But before she returned, Charlie arrived and I left.

Since I was only a part-time employee, I didn't have to work the next day. I learned later that the money in the jar had been taken. I could only imagine what was being said; the new kid on the block is usually to blame. But instead of leaving and letting the staff think I was the guilty one, I continued to work there until after Christmas. When the job ended, I never went back. To this day, I think about that woman and hope she stopped framing people for her own selfish gain.

Another memory that came to mind was a particular pool party Charlie and I had. One of our friends was a detective; he wasn't able to come to the party because he was on duty that night. He said if by chance someone called in a complaint, he would be right out. Sure enough, a complaint call did come in.

One of our male friends had been pushing me into the pool all evening, so I got fed up and called to a girlfriend to come to my aid. The pesky nuisance was relaxing in the pool, and we decided to dive in and take off his swim suit. Putting our plan into action was noisy and boisterous. Eventually, we succeeded and yelled, "We got it!"

At that very moment, one of the local policemen (not our detective friend) was looking over the fence. I threw back the trunks and went to see what the officer wanted. Our detective neighbor arrived moments later, and he and the other policeman were offered hot dogs, pop, and other food from the buffet before they went back to work. (By the way, all the neighbors had been invited, but some people just have to have something to complain about.) Before they left, the officers said that although they didn't hear much noise, we should keep the peace by bringing the party inside by eleven o'clock. So we did.

My driving reverie subsided as I approached the small town of Kamloops, British Columbia. Because it was late in the day and the sun was starting to set, I decided to exit the highway and drive into town.

I thought to myself: *I really would like to stay here and make Kamloops home.*

After I settled into the motel and had a chance to explore this place out in the middle of God's country, I knew I would be able to find a job easily, get to know some people, and make a home here. However, my friend back east had already made other arrangements. At dusk, after eating, I returned to the motel to read my book. I fell asleep, not realizing how truly tired I was.

At breakfast the following morning, I was talking to a truck driver, discussing some of the things that had happened in my life. I told him about the time I was filling up my pool after we'd had some repairs done. I thought I should clean it before the water level reached the shallow end, and so I set to the task. I was diligently working away when I slipped and hit my head and started to black out. I recall thinking: *If I don't get up, I might drown.* After falling, I remember feeling so sleepy that it was hard to function.

That feeling recalled a similar experience of when I was a child and tried to do a spin in the air while roller-skating. I took a bad fall and hit my head hard on the concrete floor of the basement, so I ran upstairs and immediately fell asleep. Later, my sister came into my room to get me, and I was in such a fog that I didn't understand who she was or what she was doing in the room. I even asked my own sister what her name was. The key to my roller skates was in my hand, and I did not know what it was for.

She asked me to come with her because Mom and Dad were waiting to take us out to dinner. When I was nestled in the car with the rest of the family, my memory returned; I remembered who everyone was and what had just taken place. After such a bad fall and severe knock to my head, I probably had a concussion. Gratefully, God sent my sister to snap me awake.

Because of that episode as a child, I told the driver, I learned to get up fast and not go to sleep after a bad fall. Following breakfast, the truck driver and I said good-bye. I left early that morning and arrived at my destination around my scheduled time of noon.

Chapter 8

Arrival

Knowing that my friend's sister was expecting me to call the minute I arrived (about noon), I tried to call her. To my surprise, there was no answer. I was still feeling butterflies in my stomach, wondering what was coming next in my life. While having second thoughts, I saw a big mall across the street. To get to the mall, I walked across a footbridge that spanned a four-lane highway. The adventuress in me just had to go and investigate.

About an hour later, I called my friends' sister again; boy was she hopping mad, wondering where I was. She acted as if it was my fault that I was an hour getting back to her when it was she who did not answer the phone when I called at the appointed time.

She gave me directions and told me to leave my car in the correct parking spot. After arriving she asked a lot of questions in a brusque unfriendly manner. I felt that she was interrogating me. This went on for about two hours before we had something to eat. She said there were stores across the street; if I wanted to go, we should get there before the rush hour. After shopping at the mall, we had supper. She prepared a big feast; she put on another big meal at breakfast the next day. I told her I wasn't a big eater. I originally thought she was doing it to impress me, especially at nine o'clock in the morning. Then she told me that my friend (her brother) had paid her in advance for my room and board. I was not a happy camper when I heard that.

The next day, she asked me if I would drive her to the other side of the city because she didn't like to drive over the bridge on her own. She had agreed to take some boxes of valuables to a friend's workplace across town, and I agreed to drive.

I had met a girl in the pool area the first day at the apartment. Her name was Joan. We'd made plans to get together to have hot dogs at the park down the street from where we lived. I told the sister about my plans and that I wanted to be back home by seven o'clock. She said it was fine with her. We were at her friend's shop for about three hours. Just as we were about to leave, we were asked to go to her friend's house for a meal. Out of a sense of duty, of course I said that I would, but I had to call Joan to tell her what was going on. Joan graciously understood and encouraged me to go for supper.

Because my friend back east was paying his sister for my room and board, I would have felt terribly guilty had I not stayed. We had started out at about two o'clock in the afternoon, and now it was going on five o'clock. So I thought we could probably make it back by seven o'clock, and I'd still have a chance to meet up with my new acquaintance.

By the time supper was cooked, however, it was going on ten o'clock. By that time, I was totally exhausted from my recent trip and hoped to leave shortly.

The sister's friend was going out of town the next day, and the sister suggested that she come back to her place so that I could cut her hair. She said I should at least do it as a favor because she had cooked such a lovely dinner for us (in other words, I should earn my meal).

I was in total shock at how people used each other, especially when someone was being paid a generous sum to be my host. I'm certain that my friend back east would have been shocked at how his sister was treating me.

I did not know my way around the sister's kitchen, and, as a boarder, I was not comfortable going into her cupboards. She suggested that I have Joan join her and a friend for dinner one night. Halfway through the dinner, one of them needed creamer for her coffee; I was asked to go to the kitchen to get it. Since I was not going to go through her cupboards to find a creamer jar to put it into, I brought the little carton of cream back to the den where we were having our meals on TV trays.

When I returned with the cream carton, she commented that if she had done that while her dad was still alive, he would send her back to put the creamer into the proper crystal jar. Then she went on and on. I guess she thought we were having a fine dining experience, but it wasn't for me. I was thoroughly embarrassed.

The next day, I moved out. I was at her place less than two weeks. I felt bad for her brother. But after everything I'd been through, my sanity meant more to me than the pay she received for having me stay there. (I had originally intended to stay with her for at least a month.)

I found a great job at an upscale shop within days of my arrival at the very same mall I visited the first day I arrived. Joan and I had discussed where I could live when the time came for me to leave my friend's sister's place. I was hoping to have more time to find a new home. But I was under stress, and it was time. My decision to leave was a fast one—too fast for me to have had an opportunity to check out the different, available, and affordable studio apartments.

Joan said it was very difficult to find a decent place to rent within my budget in the area near my work. She suggested we should be roommates. Together, we could afford to rent a two-bedroom, two-bathroom apartment with even more space. We could also get a better view of the mountains instead of the highway. The apartment she had in mind was only one floor below the penthouse. Stupid me! I trusted her, but this friendship lasted only seven months before turning sour.

I quickly discovered while living with her that I was treated like an unwelcomed guest. Everything was hers. The television was always on mute when someone called her. I had to watch what she watched. I figured out many months later that it wasn't a true friendship but a way for her to upgrade her standard of living.

She snooped in my room and checked out calls on my answering machine. I also found my mail tampered with, and then my character was put to a test. She had made friends with the sister from hell, the one I had just moved away from. A neighbor from the other end of our hallway told me she had witnessed the sister listening to our conversations from outside our apartment.

I came home early from work one day and caught Joan and the sister talking in the hallway outside our front door. Suddenly, they saw me sprinting down the hall in an effort to be on time for my son's phone call. The sister quickly went inside to hide behind the door, hoping I hadn't caught them together. The door was ajar as I entered, but to my surprise, the door wouldn't budge. I peeked around to see why. To my amazement, it was the sister trying not to be seen. By any measurement, her build was large. She had the shape of a very tall football player with broad shoulders. Their scheme to deceive me was revealed.

My roommate had shown no loyalty to me, which helped me understand why the topic of the sister from hell came up one Sunday when I wasn't working. The sister had been caught listening at our door that day. I wasn't sure how long their friendship had been going on, but I felt that it must have begun soon after I moved from the sister's place.

While doing laundry one morning, I struck up a conversation with a lady named Sara who was also doing her laundry. She was married to a man with an interesting background. He was an Indian chief and a lawyer. We became instant friends. I told her about my recent journey across the country. Since I had driven such a long distance, she suggested I get my car checked out. Heeding her advice I took my car to a small local shop for an oil change and tire rotation.

The mechanic completed the oil change and began mounting my tires. After he mounted one of the front tires and started on another, I went to the tire he had just mounted and used both of my hands to see how hard it was to move the tire. To my surprise, the tire moved and shifted from side to side. I said I didn't know a tire could move like that on a car. The mechanic took the tire off again. When he put the tire back on the car, the same thing happened. This prompted him to say that if this was his car, he would take it to the dealer. I took his advice.

At the dealership, I told the service manager about my long trip and relayed the advice the other mechanic had given me. He proceeded to check out the car. He saw nothing obvious until he got to the rear brakes and the rotor. He then noticed a large bolt missing and four other screws loose. He asked how I made such a journey safely, especially through the mountains. He also asked if the car had shimmied or if it shook when I tried to stop. My answer was that it had stopped on a dime. I said that it was a wing and a prayer that had gotten me there safely. His reply was that it had to have been just that.

I know it was a miracle to have made it that short distance from the first shop to his place of work, let alone 2,400 miles across Canada, angels had to have been beside me all the way. Now I know why I kept hearing the message to "Slow down!"

The mechanic at the dealership was very kind and gave me an old bolt until he could order a new one. The next week, I went back to have the new bolt put on my car.

Meanwhile, Sara had invited me to join her and her husband for dinner that same evening. What a beautiful time we had with fellowship, a great meal, and a perfect table setting. Not a thing could have been added. They both asked me if I would go to their church with them the following week. I asked which church they attended, and they said they were Baptist. I told them I would think about it.

Weeks went by, and I was not welcomed or treated in a very Christian way by some of the people at the Catholic Church that I had been attending. I was totally ignored for at least three weeks, and finally the priest did acknowledge me. Since he was very busy, he talked to me only briefly. I decided to give the Baptist church a try. When I went to the Baptist church with Sara and her family, I thoroughly enjoyed the service and the fellowship. So I continued to attend church with them.

The beauty shop where I had found work was very busy. My sister sent me a plane ticket to fly to the prairies of western Canada to have Christmas with she and her family, knowing that I would otherwise have been alone over the holidays. Asking for time off was not going to be easy because I had only been working there about three months. One of the workers actually asked me if I was a fugitive running from the police. I laughed and said yes; I could see why he might say that.

When I started my new job, I was so happy, smiling all the time. I hardly ever talked about my life until one of the male stylists asked me what brought me to British Columbia. Only then did I open up to him. Shortly after that conversation, he told my entire life story to my boss, which I was not expecting.

When my boss found out that I wanted time off, she told me that as a rule, everyone was to be available during the holidays—the busiest time of year. But because I had no relatives in the area, I could go to be with my family. She and her husband even drove me to the airport on Christmas Eve.

My flight was on time, and I arrived safely. The next morning, we all opened our gifts and had a great day, thanks to my sister's generosity. I even got to spend time with my other sister and her son. After a few days of a wonderful visit, I had to get back to work.

On the Sunday following my return, I went to Sara's church again, and that is when I saw the difference between the two religions. For the first time in my life, I was hearing Scripture and a real message, not just the gospel being read at me. I learned about Bible studies. Then, between Bible classes and the service, the church had cookies, coffee, tea, and soft drinks where the people from the early service and the people from the service about to begin were able to congregate and fellowship together. It was warm, welcoming and friendly and I was totally impressed. I then asked if I could begin going with them on a regular basis. It wasn't just because they knew everyone but because everyone was made to feel special. I was new to the city and wanted to meet more Baptists.

Chapter 9

New Beginnings

A FEW WEEKS WENT BY, and I took every opportunity to go back to a church service with my friends. After the service, we went to the fellowship room. I had a little cross on my coat. New people were given these crosses so that members would know they were from other places and could stop and talk. This time, I was waiting for the crowd to get by me when a man—also wearing a cross—started a conversation with me. He was from the Midwest in the United States, and he asked me where I was from. This conversation was the beginning of a real friendship and later a relationship.

For privacy's sake, I will refer to him as "John." He was staying in the big city for a few days on business. He asked me to lunch the next day. The plan was for me to bring dressy clothes because we would be doing casual things during the day. He had planned something special for the evening.

I went into my closet, which was dark, to get all my things for the day and grabbed my shoes to go with my navy blue Jones of New York suit to wear that evening. Not realizing it, I took the same style of shoe—one black and one blue. I didn't notice the shoes were different colors until I put them on for our dinner date. Thank goodness, I was wearing my good casual shoes that looked okay with the outfit. I certainly was embarrassed.

The evening went well, and the meal was out of this world. The restaurant was high up in the hotel, above the city, with a great panoramic view.

The next day, John had some time to spend with me after he finished working. We went to the seawall because his hotel wasn't far from the bay. Just before I left to go home, John said he would call when he arrived back in the US.

By then, I was determined to go looking for my own place. Accompanied by my new friend from my apartment building, we ventured out in the morning. By noon, I had picked the studio apartment I was happy with.

I was allowed to move in early so that the next time John came on business I would not have to worry about a roommate. I could hardly believe I was finally going to be living on my own in such wonderful surroundings, having so many interesting places to explore with John.

It was pouring down rain the day of my move. The rain was so hard that my mattress would have soaked if I hadn't been able to find a plastic cover. The mattress did get wet, and the mover said, "Put your mattress upright against the wall until morning or until it dries out." What he didn't know was that it was the only piece of furniture I had to sleep on. My sofa was being delivered the next day. Happily, my mattress dried out enough to be comfortable by bedtime.

I quickly settled into my new apartment and drove all over the place exploring. One time, I met a girl who liked to hike in the mountains. We made arrangements for an outing one warm, bright spring day. Thank goodness, we left early because we started out on one trail, but before long, we ended up on another trail without even realizing it we were lost. Along came a forest ranger to save the day.

We told him we were lost and asked how we could tell which trail to take to get back to where we started. We could not see any more signs. The ranger told us to look up about ten feet. (We never would have known to look up.) He told us we were hiking on a cross-country ski trail, and the snow would be about eight feet deep in the winter. We could hardly imagine that, especially since the snow had melted in the warm spring sun. The trails were well groomed and the wildlife abundant and beautiful. We saw blackbirds and blue jays and eagles soaring high above us.

I wasn't used to working only a few days a week, and so I needed something else to do. I decided to join a fitness club and found one not far from my home. The place had a mini circuit so that a workout took only fifteen minutes. The club also had a swimming pool, a hot tub, and a steam room. When I went to use the pool one day, classes were going on. The sweet instructor, Missy, asked me to join them, and I did. After class, she and I went for coffee and became instant friends.

After a long day at work, I arrived home one evening and noticed that Missy had called. She needed to see me and asked when I could get to her place. When I got there, she was doubled over. I quickly put Missy and her children in my little car and headed to the nearest hospital. She had to stay there until the results came in. The nurses told me to take the children home because the test results would not be ready until morning.

Suddenly, here I was with three children I hardly knew. Still new to the city, I had to find my way back to her place, make the children's supper, and pack lunches for school the next day. I also helped them with their homework. I was not prepared to handle such things on short notice, but somehow I did.

The next day, I took them all to school, and then I had to remember my way back. I had called the school to say I would be picking up Missy's children and asked to have them in one place to save time. I was informed that the school was not a babysitting service. I told the school secretary that the children's mother was in surgery for a ruptured appendix and that I was from out of province. I said I would be lucky to find my way to the school to get them in such a short period of time.

When I arrived, a school staff member asked the children if they knew me. They said yes but not for very long. I asked the kids if they would please call their grandparents and tell them I had to go to work in a few days. Then I learned that their grandparents did not speak English, and the children did not speak their language, Portuguese. In the meantime, I had to wait for Missy to call them for me. When the grandparents did come for the children, it was interesting to try to communicate with them—an altogether unforgettable experience.

When I finally got back to work, my boss asked me what I had done during my time off. I told her about being a nanny over the last few days. She said I always had something funny to say, and I didn't let her down this time. She said the entire experience could only have happened to me.

A month passed and John paid another visit. We went to the library around the corner. I borrowed movies and cooked a lovely dinner, and we went for a drive up the mountains. I really did enjoy those hikes and our walks on the seawall.

John worked the whole week, and we did lots of walking in the rain forest. Some evenings, we would take walks in the little town.

After a few days, John had a surprise for me. He came to kidnap me from work. My boss had already agreed to let me have the time off. I was just finishing up with a client when John came in (unannounced) and told me to pack up my equipment; he said we were leaving. I was unaware of the plan and asked him where we were going. He told me it was a big surprise, and I would find out in time.

John was always surprising me, and I loved him for that. He told me he had arranged for us to go up the coast of Vancouver Island on a business trip. Off we went to the ferry, which took longer than expected because of heavy traffic. We did manage to be on time for the departure.

The ocean was calm, the day bright and fairly warm for late spring. This part of the trip—to get to the island by ferry—took about two hours. Getting off the ferry was not as easy as we thought it would be because we had waited for the warning signal to tell us when to be in our cars. We had parked right at the front; however, my car was not in sight. We knew we had parked it in the number one spot, right at the pillar. We did this so that we would be one of the first cars off the ferry. I went one way to look, and John went the other way.

Then, I realized I had lost both my car and John, so I went to the captain to tell him what had happened. The captain said he had sighted John and asked, "Is that your car and your friend off to the side of the pier?" Yes, it was. John had located the vehicle, waited until all the cars had driven off the ferry, drove my car onto the pier out of the way, and pulled over to wait for me.

The ferry had an A on one side and B on the other. We had the right number but the wrong side. We learned from that experience to be in our car before the warning signal went off. That way we wouldn't have had such a hard time finding our vehicle; we would avoid being embarrassed.

Driving up the coast, we came to a restaurant at the water's edge. We pulled off the road to have lunch outside on the deck and watch the waves roll in. Getting back on the road, we saw the mountains at really close range. Just seeing God's handiwork was breathtaking. Approaching a small town before our final destination, we could smell it before we could see it because the town had a paper mill. I could never forget that smell. My great uncle had a farm not far from a paper mill in the countryside in French Canada.

We still had a distance to go before we reached Painter's Lodge. When the lodge came into view, what I saw was magnificent. After we settled in, we went exploring. We saw that just down the road there were fishing boats for rent. We asked how much it was to rent a boat for just an hour. The reply was $400. I asked why it cost so much. The answer was that no boats could go out without a licensed fishing guide. Well, so much for that idea.

When John came back from work the next day, we went on a whale watch on the open sea. The weather turned wet. A misty, cold wind blew in our faces, but we saw some whales in the near distance. We were not allowed to keep the motor going because it might bother or potentially harm the whales. The law said we could only drift, which meant we would not be able to get too close to them.

On our last day, John finished work by noon. He had asked me to find something special for us to do before we left for the mainland. After calling various tours and attractions, I came across a flight tour. None was scheduled for that day. But I was told that because the mail flight had room on it, we could go on the mailman's rounds. When John came in the door, he was really surprised at what I had found. After packing our belongings and double checking to make sure we hadn't forgotten anything, we went to the nearby float docks.

The day was a bit windy, but we had lots of sunshine. The aircraft was a de Havilland Otter, and this was to be an adventure. After settling in and hearing a few instructions, we took off in a pontoon plane with floats on it so that we could land in the water. The trip was supposed to be only two hours long, but it was a bonus day for us because the pilot had to bring a logger's girlfriend back and drop off and pick up mail at a few extra places on the route.

Coming in for a landing at the dock, dogs ran up to greet us, the new passengers entered the plane, and the mail was loaded inside before another takeoff. I cannot put into words the beauty of the places where we landed. The destinations could never have been reached by car. We did twelve takeoffs and landings along the coast of the Pacific Northwest that day—truly an experience I will probably never have a chance to duplicate.

In late May, my parents came to visit; John was also coming on business. My friend and her husband and John and I were waiting for my parents to call me on my car phone, but I had cut my parents off in the excitement. Then I was in a panic. My parents did not call me right back, and I had no idea where they were. About a half hour later, they called and said they were only a few blocks away.

We went to Stanley Park to take in the sights, and then we went to the tea room in the park. Our friends took us all over the park, mostly to places I did not know about.

We had many happy moments together during the day. When John worked, my parents and I went up the mountain to have lunch in a restaurant overlooking the land extending out to the bay. From up there, we could view the sea bus and cruise ships going up to Alaska.

After lunch, we boarded a bus and then a train. We simply had to take the ride over to Westminster. We disembarked to go shopping at one of the malls. I came across a yarn store, and so I asked the lady the price of the lovely sweater in the window. The reply was an astonishing $400, so she suggested that I knit it. I was able to make the sweater for only $40. I did one sleeve in a week and the other sleeve in another week; I did the front in a week and the other side in a week. Four weeks. Not quite. Actually, it took me four years to finish the sweater. Yes, it took me only one week per section, but I would get so bored knitting that I would set it aside and come back to it later.

With John and my parents there together, the time passed quickly. We were so busy catching up with each other and going to lunch and shopping that I hardly realized when it was time for them to leave. After they left, I became homesick. And when my sweetheart left, I was on my own again.

My boss asked Bernadette (one of the ladies I worked with) if she and I would like to have tickets for a play downtown. We happily accepted and made plans to go. We had dinner at an Italian restaurant near my friend's place. We had done this several times before and had always had a great time. The tickets included meeting the actors after the play, which was fun.

When John was back in town, Bernadette took us to another place to eat down by the pier. Afterward, we took a taxi boat over to the other side because I had never done that before.

My boss's husband ran a newspaper. One day, he had a human interest/society story needing coverage but all of the reporters were assigned to other tasks. The opportunity was to cover the premier opening for a very famous Italian fashion designer's first store in North America. He asked John and me if we could take notes for him at the event. That was an experience I won't forget. My boss's husband had some suggestions on how to approach the article and asked me to find and talk to some interesting people at the event.

When we arrived I noticed a mature woman who stood out, so I ambled over to her and began a conversation. I found out she was the designer's mother. We spent the entire evening with this down-to-earth, sweet lady who honestly seemed uncomfortable with all the hoopla. She said she was glad to have some "regular" people to talk to. As it worked out, I exceeded my boss and her husband's wishes.

By the next fall, I had been living in my new place for a year. John asked me to go to the Midwest to visit his home and to meet his family. I ended up with a whole week off and got to see a little bit of the leaves in color because it was Thanksgiving.

John's family showed me many places, restaurants, and a museum in the park. He and I rented a paddleboat. When the time came to return home and get back to work, the sad good-byes seemed endless, but John said he would be back very soon.

I was just getting back to work when a call came in from John asking my boss if I could have a week off to go to Florida. To my surprise, she said yes. Again, my boss took me to the airport for this special event in my life. I think she was aware of what John was going to do.

John met me at the airport. But when I got off the plane, he seemed out of sorts. He told me he had figured out that the boat cruise my friends and I went on a few weeks earlier was a chartered cruise for single people. My friend had bought tickets for the three of us. John was definitely not pleased with me, knowing that the cruise was a mixer for singles. I had only a few friends, and yes, they all happened to be single.

He was angry with me for not having told him, and I was disappointed and upset with him too. But we went on to Florida the next day.

Arriving in Naples was a shock. The weather on the coast of southwest Florida was cooler than I had anticipated. Yes, it was December, but this was Florida—land of endless sunshine—so I naturally expected warm, sunny days, climaxing in a brilliant and eternal tropical sunset.

The reality was that in the late afternoon, as the sun began what should have been a slow, lingering descent toward the horizon, it seemed to fall much too quickly, almost crashing into the Gulf of Mexico. It took the warm temperatures with it.

Living in the Pacific Northwest, I was accustomed to the sun setting early. I rationalized that because this was the South, I could look forward to warmer, longer days. Experiencing the sun setting by 5:30 p.m. was a very rude reality check. I don't know why I thought these things other than the fact that it was Florida—the Sunshine State. As I said before, I bought into the state's marketing program.

The days were actually warm enough for sunning by the pool, but the water in the pool was too cold for swimming. The hot tub felt great though, so I certainly had no reason to complain.

John was working there in a liaison capacity and had only one presentation before a group each day. Because we were attending as the guests of his customer, we were expected to join them each evening for pre-dinner cocktails followed by dinner. Other than that, we were free to do what we pleased.

We strolled across the road to a path that led to the beach and walked. On our last evening there, the group had a clambake on the beach beside the Gulf of Mexico. The conference lasted only a few days, and my time with John seemed to go by too quickly.

When I arrived home, work kept me very busy. The weather in western Canada isn't cold, but it's always very damp, with hardly any sun in the fall and winter. The winter temperatures, however, can get cold enough to snow, and sometimes the gales become extreme in intensity.

When I returned from the trip, I had to go back and tell my coworkers that I wasn't engaged. I thought everyone was going to ask me to show off my ring. I figured John had told all the staff what his plan was. My boss called one day to tell me to stay home because the winds were strong enough to carry me off. I can understand what she was talking about because I weighed barely 100 pounds back then. Gales were forceful and consisted of persistent winds and heavy rain that pounded on the windowpanes. The storms could come up very fast, and winds could topple 300-foot redwood trees like saplings.

A few weeks went by, and John called my boss at work asking if I could go to Ontario for Christmas. John said it would be nice if we could be with my parents. She granted his request, but jokingly she encouraged me not to run off and get married.

No sooner did I get off the plane in Ontario than John proposed to me with a beautiful solitaire ring. Arriving at our hotel to celebrate Christmas, we found a beautiful fruit basket and a bottle of champagne waiting for us. What a surprise—it was the best Christmas ever!

We spent the holidays with my parents and my younger sister at the same hotel. As the day after Christmas was Boxing Day, we went shopping in one of the largest malls in Ontario and found many great sales. The next day, my family had to return home. John had to work, so we stayed a few more days. I then returned to my place on the other side of the country. I felt I was always the one having to say good-bye. Going into work the next day, I had the greatest time saying I was truly engaged and didn't have to tell another sad story.

Several long weeks went by, and John asked me to go away with him again. He was asked to do some work for a company in Bermuda. I felt sheepish asking for more time off, but since Christmas was over it was a slow time of year. I did get to go.

Flying over the ocean and seeing the island of Bermuda for the first time, I wanted the plane to circle again just to enjoy the beautiful view and absorb the reality of what I was seeing. After landing and passing through airport customs, we retrieved our bags and went directly to our hotel.

The Princess Hotel sits high on a hill overlooking a small inlet with a pristine pink sand beach. The shallow water in Horseshoe Bay is the same beautiful turquoise I had seen from the plane earlier. Beyond the bay lay the ocean; the entire shoreline was that same shimmering color as far as the eye could see. From the shoreline, the water's color changes quickly, progressing to a deep, distinct indigo. This transition takes place quite abruptly, making it seem as though the entire island—thrust from the ocean's depths—regally floats on a ring of color. I thought there could be no other water in the world that color of blue, at least none that I was aware of then or now.

The hotel management went to great lengths to encourage guests to understand and respect the local culture and customs. Activities that we take for granted at home could be reasons for a fine or even incarceration in other countries.

We learned that during daylight hours in Bermuda, women are not allowed to wear shorts into town. Men are allowed to wear only Bermuda shorts (knee length), with socks that go to the knee and fold over. Sandals are not considered proper footwear for men or women any time of the day. Dress shoes are to be worn from late afternoon on, when people were expected to dress appropriately for dinner at a nice restaurant. This meant jackets and ties for men, skirts or dresses for women. The dress code for a pub allows a man to lose the jacket and tie, but he is still expected to wear a collared shirt. A woman can opt for trousers.

John worked most of the next day, but the rest of the week he only had to work the first few hours, so exploring we did go. Since the island was not very large, we saw all of it while we were there. We were able to enjoy some of the local culture away from the tourist routes. Because of the island's limited size, renting a car is impossible. So transport is limited to rented motor scooters or public transit. We chose to take the bus; as with everything else in Bermuda, we found it to be efficient and very clean.

We got off the bus in the downtown area of the principal city of Hamilton. It was like something from a postcard or movie set. Clean pastel buildings filled the cityscape; large, luxurious pleasure yachts bobbed gently in the harbor. We were searching for a place to eat lunch and found a tiny cafe several blocks off the main road. The locals were friendly, and the cafe served the best sandwich I have ever eaten at an incredibly reasonable price.

After lunch, we went into local shops and department stores where we purchased several woolen sweaters, shirts, and several pairs of over-the-knee socks for John. We explored the area until late afternoon, boarded the bus, and enjoyed the ride along the beautiful coast back to the hotel.

We went to dinner that evening with the group to be entertained at the King Henry VIII restaurant. The facility, staff, and band had been hired for the evening. After dinner, dancing, and more than a few rounds of drinks, our crowd became boisterous in a fun way.

Someone in our group found out that John and I were recently engaged and approached the king and his court (overseeing the festivities) to perform a mock wedding. "No!" came the answer. That went over like a lead balloon. Everyone in the party became involved in the fun of dethroning the reigning king and his court and appointing their own royals to power. We allowed the original Henry to retain his head. A new king more to the crowds' liking was appointed and crowned in an impromptu and formal ceremony.

Then everyone set to the task of marrying us. The new queen even placed her crown upon my head for the ceremony. I only wish someone had taken pictures of the entire raucous affair. We were told by the dethroned Henry (yes, he was allowed to stay if he promised to continue having fun) that it was the first time anything like it had happened in all his years at the restaurant.

We spent the remainder of our time exploring the island, St. George's town, the Bermuda Aquarium, and other attractions; in all, the week flew by too quickly. John and I had to return to our respective homes to resume work the following Monday.

When we arrived at the airport for our departure to the United States, the customs officer asked me where I was headed. I told him the first stop was in the USA, and then I was going on to Canada the following day. That is when the trouble started.

He asked, "Where are your tickets to Canada?" I explained that I had gone from Canada to John's home in the United States; it was my first stop on the way to Bermuda. I told him we were traveling together from his home and then back and that I would be returning to Canada from there the following day.

Then he asked, "Why are your tickets for Canada at John's home?" I told him I had flown there first, and

John had secured our passage from there to Bermuda and back.

He then asked, "How am I supposed to know if you are really going back to Canada not to the States to get married and stay in the country with John?" I answered, "Well, I guess I'll have to stay in Bermuda because I have no proof. I'm willing to stay here on your dime. I certainly don't have the extra money to buy a ticket to Canada."

I told him he could call my boss back home; she would confirm that I was expected to be at work on Monday morning. I must have been convincing or exasperating because eventually he let me go.

The following day, there were sad good-byes at the airport, but this time I knew it would not be long before I would see John again. This jet set dating was very costly, and all this traveling would soon have to end (especially considering the kindness my boss had shown in giving me time off from my job).

When I arrived back at work after Christmas, engaged to John, everyone knew I would eventually be moving to the United States. My boss reminded me of the promise I had made her that the wedding was not going to be rushed. It would take time before I could leave for the United States, and I would have to apply for a green card.

In late March, John was scheduled to arrive from the States in just a few days. It was then that a call came to me at night from, yes, good old Charlie. He wanted me back for a new beginning. All I could say was, "I must go now, and don't ever call me. You had your second chance, so please, don't call here again."

Now my wheels were turning, and I was beginning to panic. By the time John arrived at my place, all I could think of or talk about was how Charlie managed to get my unlisted number. Charlie and my friend's wife back east had connections with people who knew where to obtain such information. I could only guess that was how he was able to get my number. Now what?

I knew that Charlie had vacation time. He had accumulated at least four weeks—plenty of time to come my way. If he had my unlisted phone number, he probably also had my address

Chapter 10

Will Journeys Never End?

John said, "We must get you out of here fast." We determined that in late April I would move to the United States to live safely with him in a completely different world.

In mid-April, I put an "Articles for Sale" sign in my apartment building after having prayed to my Father in heaven for help. If nothing sold, I would not leave my country. Not one call came through. But when I went to work and told everyone what had happened, one person wanted this item and another wanted that one. Before long, everything sold including my car. The successful sale came just in time for me to join my fiancé when he arrived.

While John was in town, there was a party every night. One was at a hotel with all my coworkers. I will never forget my boss because of the compassion she had shown me over the two years that I worked for her. I will be forever grateful to her.

During that week, my boss invited us for dinner at her place. Another night, we went out with my friends. The final good-byes at the hotel near the Princess Line docks were bittersweet. I was leaving a job that I had loved and staff members who had become my family.

My son, my sisters, my brother, and my parents lived in Canada. This was the country of my birth. Even though I knew I would be seeing more of them (I could drive to see them from the States), this parting still made me feel very sad. But I took consolation in the fact that the possessions I couldn't take on the plane were being shipped to my new home. That gave me some comfort as I faced this separation from my family.

John had been relocated to a city about eighty miles from where I had already visited. Arriving at my new home in the Midwest, I noted that the terrain was very different from that of my hometown. The land was flat compared to the rolling hills where I grew up. The beauty of the mountains, the ocean, the parks, and the rest of the interesting new things about my most recent home made it very hard for me to leave.

Missing family and friends was hitting me faster and harder during this move than any other time I had moved. There seemed to be no one around, and people tended to keep to themselves. I did meet some of John's friends, but they were always on the go or busy with their families. We went to his boss's home for dinner some evenings, but it seemed to me that I was obligated to bring my styling scissors, because once it was learned that I was a stylist John's boss and his wife expected that service. Because he was John's boss how could I say no? It felt exactly like that earlier time in my friend's sister's apartment. I was just "earning my dinner." Being a hairstylist can sometimes seem that way.

In late spring, even for the locals it was unusually hot. Morning temperatures were in the high eighties, and by noon they were in the nineties. The weatherman told people to stay inside, not only because of air pollution but because of the extreme heat.

Not having a car was a huge adjustment for me. There were no buses near our home; even if there had been, there was no place to go. The town only had offices and a few restaurants but no local stores or boutiques in which to shop. As I eventually learned, there is nothing like the Canadian transit system in the Midwest and most of the United States—outside the largest metropolitan areas. Canadian towns and cities have buses every twenty minutes to take people shopping anywhere. In most all Canadian cities and towns, people still live right in the heart of downtown.

An example is Eaton Center in Toronto, Ontario. It is the center of a thriving downtown community, which is served by subway, streetcar, and bus transportation. Lots of people actually "live" downtown who have no need for a car and never have. It's because they have everything they need within walking distance: stores, markets, and lots of activities right in the core of the city.

I decided to get a volunteer job at a women's abuse center. While I was working one day, there was a shooting at a police station very near the center. The shooter was a man who simply decided to act out his frustrations. The whole event was very sad because one policeman who was killed had been on the force for only a year. His grandfather and father had served at the same station. To be safe, I stayed inside the secured building until John picked me up.

Sometimes, I would sit by my window in our condominium and watch my neighbor go out with her sisters and friends. That scene made me feel very lonely because I was longing to see my friends and family.

Once, when John had to go out of town for business, I prayed to my Father in heaven for a friend. Early one humid summer evening, I was taking a walk down the street and around the corner. A young boy called me over to see what he and his mom had found lying on the curb. Sadly, it was a cat that had been hit by a car; its tail was missing. The poor kitty had been dead for a while, but through that chance encounter I found a new friend, and we remain friends to this day.

Ariel became a real pal. She is an animal lover who had three dogs and a horse named Sweet Pea. She was beautiful, with chestnut coloring and the prettiest big brown eyes that always seemed to be smiling. Oh what care that horse received! I thought she would live forever.

Having Sweet Pea was quite a bit of work and expense for Ariel. Living in a condo, Ariel had to board her beautiful horse. Years later, John and I stayed at Ariel's new home and went to see Sweet Pea. The first time the horse fell seriously ill and recovered, Ariel decided to sell her. The man who boarded Sweet Pea did not allow Ariel to meet the buyer, which made all her alarms go off. She called and said she would be there with the sheriff if he didn't give her the money left owing on the sale of Sweet Pea. Eventually, she did get it. Two weeks later, Ariel received a phone call saying that the new owner wasn't able to keep the horse, so back she came.

Shortly after her return, Sweet Pea had to go to a special hospital for horses at a large university. Ariel was told that Sweet Pea had laminitis, an ailment that may have been caused from stress or from overeating in the open field. Sweet Pea was put on a diet and was not allowed to graze on grass that caused her to have difficulty with bowel movements.

Well, Sweet Pea somehow got into a pasture, ate grass, and her intestines became twisted. Then she needed a difficult and serious operation, so back to the hospital she went. Our prayers were answered, and she was able to return home.

On another occasion, Ariel had to drive to the boarding stable, load Sweet Pea into her trailer, and then drive ninety miles to the hospital—all in a blinding snowstorm—because her horse's tongue was nearly severed off near the back of the throat. I'm not sure how that happened. Sweet Pea had surgery again, and when she came back home, she took ill with colic.

My friend had to say to herself and to Sweet Pea, "You have endured enough in this life." The vet came and put her down. Sweet Pea was put to sleep and was buried by a stream in a wooded area near her home stables. She is resting peacefully.

One time, Ariel, her son, John, and I went to an amusement park for a day's outing sponsored by the company John worked for. Imagine the fun we all had getting soaking wet on the log ride, enjoying the roller coaster, and eating all the wonderful food provided. What a great day! We still talk about it.

I finally got permission to drive the company car. Being licensed in Canada, I visited the local police station with John to see how I could obtain a US driver's license. I hadn't received my green card yet, and it certainly created a problem. Yes, I needed to be licensed in my permanent state of residence, and my Canadian license was no good. The officer told me to come back with some proof of my address, and we would go from there. I called her office one morning to schedule a good time to write my exam for the license, and then I asked her when I could take my driver's test.

A week earlier, I was told that the test facility nearest our residence was under repair. I would have to go across town to take my driving test.

One day, I happened to see a driver's education instructor working with her student; they were practicing a backing procedure between four orange cones—two on one side and two more on the other. I stopped and asked her if I could try it out. I told her that I was from another country, and I needed to take the driver's test soon. She graciously let me use the cones and asked that I stay with the cones while she took her student out for a drive.

I had to perform the backing up maneuver without turning to look out the rear window, using only my mirrors (like a truck driver). I kept hitting the cones. I couldn't get the hang of using my mirrors to back up because I was never taught that method.

John was out of town, so I called the police station to see when I could take my driver's test. The police officer said any time that morning would be fine. When I arrived to take my written exam, the instructor told me to have a seat and then had me take the exam. I was caught completely off guard when she told me that after I finished she would have time for my driving test. The construction workers hadn't started the repairs on her facility yet. This was a surprise because I didn't feel that I was ready, so I sent up some quick "911 prayers" to God.

I completed the written exam and nervously approached the driving test, knowing that just a few days before I had touched those orange cones but hadn't knocked them down. I got in the driver's seat and was ready to go. With anxious feelings and my seat belt on, I watched the instructor go around the car. She went to the front and then to the back. Then she repeated the movement, came to my window, and said we couldn't go. I asked why. She had me get out of the car and showed me that the registration stickers on the plates had expired.

I opened up the glove box and found that John had neglected to put the current stickers on. I asked the officer if those were the right stickers, and she said they were. She told me if I could get them on within ten minutes, we could still go out for my test.

I didn't realize we had a plastic protector over the plates, with four rusted screws holding it together. I walked over to the building next door and asked if I could borrow a screwdriver. I could not get the coverings off. Trying to unscrew the rusted screws was not an easy task, so I pried the covering apart, squeezed my fingers under the cover, and put one sticker on the front plate and one sticker on the back. If I wasn't able to get them on, all I could think of was that we would be in big trouble with the law.

I noticed the surprised look on the officer's face when I returned to her office. She asked me how I had accomplished the job so quickly because she saw that the screws were rusty. She seemed pretty confident that I would not complete the task on time.

She had me go through the cones first. Praying all the way, I passed without touching a single cone. Thank God; my nerves wouldn't have been able to withstand a repeat test. So I had great news for John when he returned home from his trip. And with a valid driver's license, with photo identification I was also able to obtain a library card.

Going to the airport to pick up John, I found my way easily because I was used to driving in new cities on my own. I got caught in a traffic jam and was beginning to think that I wouldn't have time to get there before he landed. Luckily, I made it, but John's flight ended up being delayed for a total of seven hours. When he finally arrived home, we were thankful for his safe trip and didn't concentrate on the negative setbacks. We went out to celebrate my new driver's license.

Then I began the nightmare process of applying for a green card. John and I went to my hometown for the first time since I had left the Pacific Northwest. I stayed with my family, and John went to work. During that stay, I helped my younger sister move and rearrange her furniture. I called Mulligan to ask him to come for a visit. But as soon as he left, good old Charlie drove by. I guess he was following my son that day.

My sister and I put sheets on the window for privacy until she could hang proper draperies. Outside the window were some overgrown shrubs, and we didn't want anyone looking inside. After having worked all day, we were tired and went to bed.

Around midnight, we heard a harsh banging on the bedroom window. The instant fear I felt was something that cannot be put into words. Then the intruder (or intruders) went to the back door. I ran for the phone and dialed 911. Someone answered on the first ring, and I tried to explain to that person what was happening. But because I was so distraught, I wasn't making any sense. Fear had overtaken me to the point of confusion; I wasn't able to put a sentence together. So my sister took over the call. I guess I went into some form of shock because I couldn't talk, and the banging continued.

When the police came, we found out it was only my sister's boyfriend, wanting to pick up some beer he had forgotten earlier that day. He decided to come by that night—a poor choice. What an evening! He did say he was sorry when he saw how panicked we were.

After a few weeks, John came, and we went back home to the Midwest. We were still working on my divorce, which finally came through the following year (September 1995). The entire undertaking cost just under $500 because we bought the divorce kit from a store. I wish I had been aware of that information before I hired a lawyer years earlier. It would have been so much cheaper and easier on my humble income. The following March, John and I were married.

Three months after the wedding, John was offered a position with the company's Canadian division. After talking it over with me, he accepted it. We would be living and working in Ontario's key metropolitan city. Now it was his turn to try out a new country. We had two weeks to find a place to live before he started work.

A lovely real estate lady, who later became a friend, took us all over the city to look for a suitable, affordable house. When we weren't able to find one in our price range, she told us she knew a man who owned a townhouse. After some negotiations, he rented the condo to us.

Our new home was in a lovely Victorian part of town. When we originally went to see it, the realtor said, "Oh look, you could put your sofa in this part of the living room." We replied, "Yes, if we had one to put there, we would." We could only laugh because I don't think she'd ever dealt with clients who owned hardly any furniture. We eventually bought the condo from the landlord.

Before our move away from the Midwest to Canada, we experienced a humorous encounter. Following the church service one day, our congregation gave us a going-away lunch party at a pizza restaurant. After lunch, a young woman came to us and said that she and her family were going to Sudbury, Ontario in a few weeks to visit some friends and go skiing. We both looked at her and invited her to come with us outside and see how hot the weather was that day—about ninety degrees. We told her it gets almost that hot in Ontario, and they would not be able to ski on their trip since there would be no snow.

I can only imagine the looks on the faces of the security people at the border when visitors show up during the summertime with ski equipment on top of their cars. If they aren't informed about the weather in Canada that time of year, they pack a crazy wardrobe and are terribly embarrassed. Believe it or not, customs officers here told us this happens frequently.

The day came for us to move to Canada. Our real estate man came to the condo around noon to see if all was well, but it wasn't. The moving truck had broken down coming in from another state. We'd been waiting on another truck, which had just pulled up, so the delay put stress on everyone. Our deadline was to be out of the house by 4:00 p.m.; otherwise there would be a fine to pay.

Our realtor came back a few hours later. We still had lots of items to load into the truck because the inventory for customs was taking up a lot of time. Each box, piece of furniture, and loose item had to be labeled with a barcode sticker and listed on a corresponding worksheet. The men were doing all of this as they loaded the truck, but the little details were causing a problem.

Before the move date, I thought I would sell some of the items we really didn't need in Canada. When I went to sell my spare bedroom furniture, the woman who came to see it decided she wanted to buy all John's furniture—even things that weren't for sale. She wanted my dining set, and although it was my prize possession, I sold it to her. It was a hard thing to do because it was really expensive. To replace it would have cost around $3,000 at one of the finer stores in Canada. That night, we went to buy a new dining set so that we would have something to eat on when we settled in.

A few years went by, and I was shopping with John in a very busy part of downtown when he heard my name being called. He asked me if I knew the lady who called my name three times. The lady was my dear friend Marley. Even though I talked to her on the phone, I hadn't let her know that I'd moved back to Canada. I was not ready to talk to her in person yet.

What were the odds that, in a greater metropolitan area of eight million people, she would run into me? When she found out I had been in the area for quite a while, I had some explaining to do. She was aware of my fears from the past and forgave me, knowing how Charlie and a few friends had been after me in a bad way.

Marley and I had some catching up to do. We went to cafes and the movies and shopping; we did lots of activities together. One time, we ventured on the Grayline bus to Hamilton for the day, stopping at a tea room to have lunch. We went into many antique places and down to a park and even to a castle.

When it was time for me to find work, I found a part-time job at a beauty supply shop. During that time, a friend from our church came and told me that she already had a stylist, but when her regular stylist was out of town (or off), she would like me to fill in. Not even a year had passed when she asked if I would consider working at her nursing home as a stylist for the residents (her stylist was going on vacation). I did, and when her stylist retired the next year, I was able to step in and take her place.

One Sunday, our pastor suggested that John should consider taking a vacation. Being a typical man, my husband ignored the advice. Well, three weeks went by, and there had been no holiday. Soon thereafter, however, John was hospitalized for five days with a very serious infection. The Lord gave John the time off he needed. God often uses others to tell us what we are supposed to do. Even though my husband endured many setbacks, his faith never wavered.

Casey, another of my childhood friends, came to visit me with a neighbor friend of hers. Then Casey and her husband came, and we went to see the fireworks at the downtown harbor. It was called a Festival of Lights. We went out to a restaurant where we sat on the roof and had an excellent view of the fireworks.

What a show they put on that evening! The colors and the patterns of the fireworks were indescribable. Everyone was in awe. The crowds had thinned out, and we were leaving. When we passed a street vendor selling hot dogs and polish sausage, Casey's husband just had to have a polish sausage with sauerkraut on a bun. Crowded into the car on the way home the smell of the garlic in the polish sausage really got our attention. I'm guessing Casey had to leave the windows open all night.

One winter's night in a small town close to us, the town's little-theater company hosted a murder mystery party. It was staged on a historic railroad that was still operating, and we just had to go. John finished work by five o'clock. Since it was snowing, we had to hurry to get to the train because we had a forty-minute drive to get there if good weather conditions held. As we traveled north, the weather worsened by the minute, and we wondered if the event would still take place. By the time we arrived, the snowdrifts between us and the train were so high that we needed a boost to get on the train.

When we got on board, the train was just beginning to get warm inside. The frost on the windows and the blowing snow made it almost impossible to see anything outside. It really did seem like a polar express ride

Our trip was delayed for over an hour as we waited for others to make it to the station on that cold, snowy evening. Finally, everyone who was able to make it did, and we got on our way. Unfortunately, this was their very first try at a mystery party and the timing was not yet perfected to coordinate its climax with arriving at the cafe for dinner. By the time we reached the little cafe it was already 9:30 p.m., and we were still into the mystery. With all the delays, and the actors attempting to speed up the production the mystery was getting very mixed up. By the time our food came, everyone was quite hungry. But the food was cold and overcooked. (I'm sure the meal had been ready long before it was served.)

The entire program was supposed to last until nine o'clock, but it was eleven o'clock when we finished eating. The party and the trip back to our departure point was fun, but we were all exhausted when we finally rolled into the station.

Driving home was not easy because by then the roads were covered with a thick ice base and about a foot of fresh snow. We arrived home well into the early morning hours and fell into bed.

I prayed their next mystery party would be more successful.

Christmas was coming, and our little Victorian village was having a Christmas parade with carolers in Victorian costumes. The town was lit up with candles. Sidewalk vendors sold hot cider and hot chocolate, and all the boutique stores stayed open until midnight. Since this was to be a very special event, we asked our family to join us.

Mom and Dad came for Christmas Eve, and Mulligan came on Christmas Day. We always spent our holidays with my family because of how difficult it was to get to John's family in the Midwest that time of year. His children went to be with his former spouse's parents. New Year's was very difficult because the same thing happened. We would go to where they lived, stay at a hotel nearby, and see them for only a few hours.

We did get to visit his sister's family one Christmas. John's nieces and nephew joined us, and we all had a good time. On our trip back to Canada, however, we found the roads terrible. We passed a horrible accident with a twenty-car pileup. Had we been at that location a few moments earlier, we'd have been involved too. We had to stop traveling in winter because of the weather and the short visits, so we decided to visit John's family only in warmer weather.

When Mother's Day arrived Mom and Dad came to visit. Mom and I went to our church, which was having a mother/daughter banquet. The day after the banquet, I became ill. Mom and Dad decided to go home earlier than planned. After they left, I became really sick with a bad flu; I could keep no food or water in me. On the third day, the doctor made a house call. He said that if I wasn't better by the next day, John should to take me to the hospital. The doctor told me to take ice chips and suck on them all day so that I wouldn't get dehydrated. He said dehydration is the number one killer with the flu. I was to avoid big gulps of water, which came back up, and just let water drip down my throat—much like an IV drips into the body. With his advice, I did get better.

On Friday nights, we hosted a Bible study in our home and sometimes at a friend's place. One night when it was our turn, I was cooking a nice dinner. I placed an empty Pyrex dish on one of the burners because the kitchen had limited space and I was in a hurry. When I went to take the dish off the burner, I realized the burner was hot. I grabbed an oven mitt to move the hot empty dish to another burner and when the heated casserole dish touched the cold burner hot glass exploded everywhere. I was in my bare feet, standing on a floor covered with burning hot glass fragments, but my angel was beside me. No pieces hit my feet, my eyes, or my face, and only a very small area on the tile floor melted from the heat of the broken glass. Fortunately, all of the food was still in the oven, and thankfully our meal was not ruined. Another angel was there.

Two friends from my hometown were coming to visit, one of whom was Casey. She and I had been friends since lower grade school. The day before they arrived, my car malfunctioned right in front my car dealer's place of business. The tie rod underneath my car had come off. Thankfully, the part was still under warranty.

The day I was to pick up Casey and her friend, the weather was terrible, with wind, ice, and snow. Because my car was in the shop, I had to take a bus to meet them at a mall (the bus station is attached) not far from my home. Two buses later, I caught up with them and told them what had happened. Somehow, I managed to get onto the wrong bus going home. We had to get off at a major stop and transfer to another bus that would get us home.

Imagine standing on the wet, snowy surface, with the wind and snow blowing in our faces while we waited with suitcases for a bus. It finally came, but was far behind schedule because of the weather. When we finally reached my place we were certainly ready for some hot tea.

The next day, we went to our little village to shop at the boutiques, and we went afterward to another mall. We always had so much fun and so many good meals when they visited that my friends called it my "bed and breakfast."

Marley and I often went to the movies when I stayed at her place in the big city. We had some great times together. Going downtown to the trendy areas was always a very special time. We would spend time shopping the boutiques and enjoying the restaurants and galleries. We would go to her work place and then go shopping. We visited Center Island to see all the old Victorian cottages by the lake. We even rented a bicycle for two and explored the island. We also went to the tearoom there.

A few months later, I was experiencing tooth pain, so I went to the dentist. After the x-rays were developed, the dentist explained that I needed to have the tooth filled. But unfortunately, the filling was so close to the root that he might need to perform a root canal.

A week later, I went for the procedure. While the dentist was working on my tooth, I started praying. I asked my Father in heaven to help me with the anxiety of having to go through the pain—not to mention the expense of a root canal. I was resting that evening at home when my dentist called to see how my pain was. I told him I had no pain, and I was feeling pretty good. Thanking him for his call, I could tell in his voice that this kind of result seemed unbelievable to him. I did not require any surgery. Thank you, Jesus.

Another summer came and went. As autumn approached, John and I decided to go for a Thanksgiving weekend getaway. We went to a resort in the habitable part of North Ontario. The drive was good, but the weather turned wet, damp, and very cool.

On Friday night, we sat by a big burning fire in the lodge and then went back to our room to read. The next day was a bit chilly, but the sun was shining. So we took a paddle boat out on the lake and tried to get some pictures of the loons playing in the water. That evening we enjoyed a great meal at the resort and had good conversations with the other guests.

We went for a walk in the woods the next day. With my new camera in hand, I started clicking away. Through my lens I saw a lonely, soft green maple leaf with water drops facing me. This leaf was lying on other colorful leaves. Putting my camera on manual mode, I started clicking away and then moved on to my next subject.

While going through our pictures at home, John came across the maple leaf picture. It was my first time out using a quality camera, and I'd never taken a lesson. We realized I had a hidden gift from God. That particular picture turned out so well that John took it to a studio and had it blown up and framed; he surprised me by giving it to me at Christmas. I will always remember the kindness of his gesture.

As Christmas drew near, we were getting ready to go to John's Christmas party late one Saturday afternoon. My son called to tell me that he and his girlfriend were coming for a visit. About forty minutes later, they arrived and told us a baby was on its way around June. Then they announced they were getting married.

It was all great news. Mulligan was now thirty years old and had seemed happy in the bachelor role. I had almost given up hope of ever being a grandmother. We all went out to supper to celebrate the wonderful news.

My grandson was born in June, one day before my own birthday. What a little darling he is. I got to see him every other weekend, which was such a joy.

One day at work, one of our nursing home residents was getting her nails done. After her nails dried, it was time for me to wash and blow-dry her hair. She was in a wheelchair, and one of her hands was crippled with severe arthritis. On that particular day, she was telling me that all she wanted in life was to be able to cut her own meat at dinner. I asked her if she believed in Jesus Christ, and she said she did. I then began to pray with her for that small request from our Father in heaven. Suddenly, her hand began to open up like a bud in blossom. I then called out to the other girl and asked her if the lady's hand had been closed when she had done her nails. I said, "Look at her hand now." We had witnessed a small miracle, and we all cried in thanksgiving to our heavenly Father.

Months later, my friend Casey called to ask if she and her friend could take me to Niagara-on-the-Lake (a small resort town on the Canadian side of the Niagara River) as a thank you gift for having both of them at my home (the "bed and breakfast"). I was to pick them up at the bus station the next week. On my way there, the newscaster came on and said that one of the Twin Towers in New York City had just been hit by a plane. Like so many other people, I thought: *What a tragic accident!* Not long afterward, the news came that the other tower had been hit, and more attacks had occurred in other parts of the US. I picked up my friends and told them what had happened. We rushed to my place to watch the news. What a shock! We were trying to decide whether or not to go on with our plans. Since our reservations were already paid for, we went.

When we arrived at our destination, a few Americans were also staying at the inn. To say the least, they were shocked. We comforted them as best as we could. They repeatedly said how much they appreciated our thoughtfulness. Because the borders were all closed, they weren't able to return home for a few days.

We went out for supper and then did a bit of shopping. The stores closed early during the week nights in this particular tourist destination. The next day, we went to the falls and had a late dinner. Then we did more shopping before going back to the inn.

The truck traffic going to the States was something to see. Because of the attacks, border security had been tightened at all crossings, and the lines extended for miles. Later, a plan to blow up the bridge spanning the Niagara River was discovered and prevented.

People lived in great fear about what might happen next, but everyone tried to go on with normal life. After a few days, we went home and prayed at the church for our neighbors in the United States. Every year on September eleventh (9/11), I remember the Americans we met and for whom we prayed.

At the little church we attended in the Victorian Village, we were getting ready for our Christmas morning service. John and I were singing in the choir. My parents came down for the Christmas play. The little ones were so cute that they stole the show.

On a very warm, sunny day in the late winter of 2002, Shirley asked me to go skiing with her. I loaded up the car with cross-country ski gear and set out to pick her up; then off we went. Most of the afternoon was warm, but it was getting even warmer late in the day, though not enough to melt the snow.

After having traversed the trails for a couple of hours, we decided to go one more round before leaving. Down a hill I went, but this time my right ski went one way, and the left ski went the other. Because the skis were crossed, I fell down very hard. Trying to stand up, I quickly realized I couldn't. I knew I had seriously damaged my left knee and couldn't stand without support.

My friend went looking for the ski patrol, and they found me off the prepared trail. I was crawling across a field of deep snow on my hands and knees, using my skis as snowshoes to keep me atop the soft, deep snow.

When the ski patrol arrived, I was boosted up onto the snowmobile and taken to my car. The patrolman had to help me into it. I was able to drive because it was the left knee that was damaged.

When I got home, I left my equipment in the car and crawled up all the outside steps to the outer door. Then I negotiated the inside steps going up to the bedrooms. When John heard me crawling up the stairs (thump-drag, thump-drag, thump-drag), he was shocked. He asked me what I had done, and I told him the whole sad story.

With his help, I managed to get into bed. By putting a heating pad on my knee, the pain lessened, but the swelling got much worse. A few hours later, John took me to the hospital because my knee had swollen up like a balloon.

The doctor in the emergency room told me I would have to come back in about two weeks; the swelling needed to go down significantly before he could x-ray it properly. Leaving the hospital with a brace from my ankle to my upper thigh and wobbling on crutches, I knew the recovery from this accident was not going to be easy.

On Monday, I went to work on crutches to cut and style hair. One lady, who came to the shop in a wheelchair, commented that it must not be a good day for me. I stayed for half the day, but standing up was painful and tiring.

A week later, I began physical therapy. After a few days, the therapist was measuring the radius of my knee as she pushed lightly on it. We discovered it was stiff and had little give. A week later, she pushed my knee down straight; it was almost touching the bed. When she did that, I nearly saw stars. She said she had done me a favor because if the patient does not do the exercises after a knee injury, the hamstring can seize up.

At the time, I was not happy with the pain, but now I wish I could thank her because, thanks to her exercises, I am able to bend my knee all the way down and back. I now have full range of motion in my knee.

When I went back to the doctor, new x-rays showed the ligament in my left knee was torn. He said I should have it operated on. I told him I'd had many prayers said for me in this country and in the United States. I also showed him that I could bend my knee up, go down stairs, and ride a bike. So I said no to the operation. Thank you, Jesus, for your healing hands.

Six weeks after my fall, we visited Hawaii with friends. While exploring the area, John and I went on a switchback path down a cliff to get to the black beach—a feature of the Big Island—formed by the sea wearing down volcanic rock into a fine black sand. I climbed back up the cliff with no knee problems whatsoever, and I must say that the beach was something to see.

Our friends had access to a timeshare. We split the expense so that it didn't cost either couple too much. They explained to us about their timeshare program and suggested we go and listen to their sales talk and take advantage of any free offers. The timeshare unit was indeed lovely. It was a furnished, full-sized condo with a fully-equipped kitchen. All we had to do was buy the groceries we would need during our stay.

On the evening we arrived, the facilities management staff held a reception and gave a presentation about the island and the current attractions. They emphasized that if a visitor was interested in any activity or tour, he or she needed to put an order in early because some filled up quickly.

When we went to the nearest town of Kona, we found plenty of opportunities to attend timeshare presentations; all of them offered two free tickets for various tours. So, early in the trip, we sat in on some timeshare presentations to get the free passes. Our friends went to a few, and we went to different ones. That way we got to go on more tours at reduced prices. We also learned that the presentations were sometimes full. But if we were scheduled for that presentation, they would still give us the free passes for the tour attraction.

Our favorite activity was snorkeling in the shallow bays. Unlike the deeper water that diffused light and color, the shallow water allowed us to experience all the brilliant colors of the coral reef and the fish. All I could say was, "Wow!"

We took a two-hour plane ride over the mountains to see dormant and active volcanoes. We flew close to the crater's rim of the active volcano and looked down into the yellow-orange soup of molten lava. The pilot flew us past a small house on the side of the mountain, which was surrounded by streams of molten flowing lava. It was almost unbelievable that the homeowners stayed on their property, considering all the violent geological activity taking place around them. Then the pilot flew low along the coastline where we could see the orange river of lava creating great clouds of steam as it oozed into the sea.

The next tour was a breathtaking sunset cruise. It included all the food we could eat and an unlimited supply of Mai Tais—all of which we took advantage.

Another tour included an evening at one of the largest cattle ranches in the world. The hosts served us a chuck wagon barbeque meal, provided cowboy entertainment, and gave tours of the ranch. It was located near the summit of a long-extinct volcano. Getting to the location by way of a narrow, steep road was a task for our poor vehicle of a bus. The tour guides were actual cowboys on the ranch who explained how the ranch came about, gave a little history about the family, and provided facts about the cattle raised there and sent all over the world to breed.

After we ate, we listened to some cowboy songs and tried our hand at roping as the sun slipped into the sea. The ranchers had put in a full day, and they had to be up at dawn. It was time for us to leave.

The bus ride back down the mountainside was scary. We could feel the stress the brakes were under as they were being pumped. We could feel the tension inside. The quiet bus descended the steep incline, negotiating the curves on the narrow mountain road until we reached level ground. It was the ride of our lives.

The next day, we went on a submarine excursion to see fish of all sizes and colors and the coral reef in the shallower water. The scenery was fascinating. But as we travelled down and settled on the seafloor in about 110 feet of water, everything turned deep blue. That experience remains a very fond memory, especially when the bigger fish came up to the large oval window of the submarine and stared at us. What a thrill!

Our next big attraction was an awesome Hawaiian luau. The tables were set up just off the beach and were loaded with an amazing variety of exotic food. A whole pig, wrapped in banana leaves, had been cooking in a hand-dug pit for twenty-four hours. Some of the local natives rowed to shore in dugouts—some were the same people who prepared the meal. They explained the contents of the luau and the preparation of the local foods. Then they served us and even entertained us with a fire dance that seemed never ending; it was certainly a highlight of our trip.

Our ten days were coming to a close, so we toured the entire Big Island one last time. We stopped at a macadamia nut plantation and packaging factory. Going further up the mountain, we came to a lava desert and walked on the blackened lava. A Hawaiian myth says to take nothing back with you because it is bad luck.

Going from Kona on one side of the Big Island to Hilo on the other side—via the mountain route—took us through seven of the eight climates on planet earth. The weather was hot down at sea level. But as we traveled up the mountain, we entered the rainforest. There were even lava deserts that mimicked the climatic conditions of the high desert on the mainland. The higher elevations sometimes got snow.

The day before leaving, we went on a four-hour snorkeling trip to a coral reef out in the Pacific. We had a half-hour ride to the site and then went snorkeling. We then enjoyed a lunch prepared by the tour guides. What a picnic it was: fresh pineapple, lovely sandwiches, and dessert.

After our break, we went back in for more snorkeling. We even got to see a nine-foot shark resting under a coral overhang about eight feet below us.

On the ride back to Kona, we saw some spinner dolphins swimming rapidly alongside us. As they swam, they leaped out of the water, spinning and plunging back into the sea. It was definitely a memorable experience.

When our ten days were up, it was time to return to work. We said sad good-byes to our friends who stayed on for the full two weeks. We were on the way to the airport to catch our plane but had to stop at the primary tourist island of Oahu. We were transferring there to a larger plane to take us back to Ontario.

We made good use of our three-hour layover by going to see the *USS Arizona* at Pearl Harbor. The procedure for boarding the boat took us across Pearl Harbor, and the line to see the sunken warship was organized by numbers and the color of our ticket. So many people were present that day that I wasn't sure if we could see the ship in the short amount of time we had. However, we did get to see that somber memorial and made it to the airport in good time to catch our flight.

Back home, things were not going well for John at work. The company required all the sales reps to sell a service to their top two accounts that was known not to work properly. John had sold a completely new computer system to his top two accounts that year. He refused to risk his relationship with his customers. The company insisted. John resisted, and so he began looking for a new job.

I went to a women's retreat a week after our return from Hawaii. This retreat started on a Friday night, and at least thirty women from our church attended.

At the retreat, I was talking with a lady who was an assistant to operating room doctors. Being curious, I asked her which operation was most frequently performed at the hospital. She said it was knee surgery. When I told her I had experienced a knee injury, she asked me how many years ago. When I told her it had been only eight or nine weeks, she said my rapid healing had to have been a miracle. People who'd had surgery a year ago didn't have the flexibility I had shortly after my accident. In my heart, I knew it was a miracle.

My acquaintance from the church, my friend Sal and I called ourselves "the three musketeers" because the three of us went shopping, played tennis, and frequented tea rooms together. On one such occasion, my mom joined us, and we all went to an old mill that had been turned into a restaurant for a traditional high tea. Arriving fifteen minutes early, the host instructed us to have a seat in a side room because we were fashionably early (meaning, how rude of us to have shown up so soon).

As we were being seated, the menus were passed around, and my mom decided to be adventurous. She asked for the Russian tea. What a taste! The tea was almost oily and tasted like a mixture of hot water and hickory smoke. I asked for an English tea for my mom, knowing the tea she ordered was not for her. We all wanted to enjoy this wonderful experience. But the look on the waiter's face told me that he was not pleased.

The high tea was great. The three-tier decorator plate had small sandwiches cut into quarters with the crust removed. They were made with cucumber, salmon, and ham and cheese. The next tier had scones with Devonshire cream and fresh preserves for toppings. The top tier was for the small desserts. What a lovely experience; I would go again in a minute.

We took the subway home, which was an adventure for my friend Sal. This was her first trip going outside her section of town via subway. Her usual mode of transportation to this side of town was by car. The day's adventure included various transfers on the subway system. I was impressed that Sal was using the city transit.

I also sometimes had high tea for my friends. Putting out my Irish linens, candles, and my best china from Germany and France, I baked homemade scones, made mock Devonshire cream, and served homemade preserves. These dishes always made those afternoons a great success.

My friend Sal had a lovely backyard with a pool. She called this site her English garden because it reminded her of her native home back in England. In September, Sal invited a friend of mine and me to her place for a garden lunch, which was so delicious. She served us delicate sandwiches, delectable desserts, and English tea. We were surrounded by her roses of pinks and yellows, along with white daisies—all set against the backdrop of the pool. We all had a great time.

In October, Sal became very ill. I went often to her house to help her in any way I could. The stubbornness in her character was unbelievable. It was obvious that she was becoming weak and disoriented. I said, "You are so sick; please let me take you to the hospital." Her answer was always no.

During one visit, I wanted to call an ambulance, but she declined. The emergency medical service personnel cannot force someone to go to the hospital if they don't want to go. I told her that if she was still not better by morning, I would get John to help lift her into the car and take her to the hospital. I thank God her daughter came in the morning and saw how sick her mother was.

Sal relented and allowed her daughter to take her to the emergency room. There, Sal's daughter discovered that if she had waited a few more hours to take her mother to the hospital, Sal probably would have died from dehydration.

Sal was hospitalized for months, and the nurses thought she would never leave the hospital. Through prayer and her belief in God, she was able to go home. She had a rare disease called Wagner's, which is something like lupus. However, it can go into remission—the stage it is in now.

At first, Sal was confined to a wheelchair. She then moved on to a walker, and now she is completely mobile and in better health than most people her age. She is driving and having a good time. She recently traveled overseas to see her family and has made other trips in and out of Canada. What a miracle!

During this time, we had our pastor, his family, and some mutual friends over for a big turkey dinner, which I served on fine china. I wanted everything to be just perfect. I only wished I had served it on dishes that were dishwasher safe. I spent so much time cooking and cleaning up that by the time I did get to sit down, the pastor had to leave. This reminded me of the story in the Bible about Martha and Mary. Sometimes it takes personal experience to relate to God's calling to establish proper priorities.

Another Christmas came; this time it presented us with sad news. Mulligan's fiancé told us she was not going to marry my son. When I asked her why, her answer was that she wanted a house before she reached the age my son was at that time. Well, thank goodness they never married because she really did not love Mulligan. Her focus was on material things, but I do hope she finds what she is looking for in a partner.

The pressures at John's workplace were becoming difficult; they had doubled his quota because he had already achieved 100 percent of it halfway through the year. While we were at a church function, a man who was getting to know John mentioned that the company he worked for was looking for more help. John contacted the director and was invited to go for an interview. They offered John the job and said he could start in two weeks. Prayers were answered once again.

Being responsible for managing one of the company's business units, John set to the task. He found in his analysis that no proper accountancy was in place for his unit. Three months after starting, he had to go to his boss and explain to her that the financials were not correct. The exposed margin between what was supposed to be and what was factual was significant. His analysis was thorough, and his accounting audit was complete.

She had hired a consultant to provide vision and direction on business opportunities. But in a year's time, between the director's flagrant expenses and the new consultant's fees, the entire department's budget had been grossly exceeded. Due to poor business practices and inaccurate accountancy the entire business department had to be sold. Sadly, all the employees in that department—not just in John's division—lost their jobs.

Chapter 11

Moves, Moves, Moves

AFTER THAT EXPERIENCE, JOHN WAS back to pounding the pavement. We offered up more prayers, and he found a great job. He was hired by an e-business company headquartered in the Pacific Northwest and would be working in Michigan where his auto manufacturer customers were located.

Since we owned our condo, I couldn't go with him until it sold. Eventually, he would be transferred back to the Midwest and we would move simultaneously from our home in Ontario and from John's apartment in Michigan. Until then we would alternate commutes, and that was actually fun.

Before moving I had a frightening mishap. Starting my drive to work one day, I pulled out of our garage, and my car was suddenly heading right for my neighbor's garage door. No matter how hard I pushed on the brake pedal, it wouldn't stop. I cried out to Jesus, "Please stop this car!" My car had obviously developed brake problems. With faith, I asked my Father in heaven to help get my car to the garage without any mishaps. I made it safely because it was very early in the morning, and there was minimal traffic. The repair shop was close enough that I was able to walk the rest of the way to work and back to the shop to pick up my car after work.

Because the city where John now lived was on the Canadian border, I was able to travel by train to see him every other weekend, and he came to Ontario on the alternate weekends.

During one of those trips, I traveled first class. I asked my Father in heaven to give me wisdom and to use me on the journey. No one sat beside me at the first stop. The next station rendered the same result. I was beginning to think that the Lord had other plans for me that day. However, at the last stop before our destination, a young man came and sat with me because it was the only available seat. I could only wonder why the Lord brought me this particular person. I was thinking to myself that this handsome young man would have probably preferred sitting with a very young, pretty girl—not a lady in her mid-fifties. I could have been his mom or even his grandmother.

My meal was coming, so to start a conversation I told him that I was not very hungry. I suggested that he take what he liked, explaining that because of a two-hour delay on my last trip I was able to travel first class. The meal was included with my fare. This was a great opening to a conversation that lasted the rest of the trip. He was hungry, and we had about three hours left to go.

I asked him what courses he was taking at college and what his plans were after graduation. To my surprise, he didn't really know. The wisdom that I had prayed for so recently came spilling out. I asked him about his hobbies, and he told me that he liked theater, journalism, and photography. I suggested that he consider doing something with journalism and photography. He could start by interviewing friends, with a camera on hand. He could use a video camera to capture them doing what they do best. He might get permission to publish the interviews in the school newsletter.

Then I suggested that he volunteer at some of the theaters in town. He could take that same technique of doing interviews at his school and do the same thing for the theaters featured in the local newspaper.

Before we knew it, our destination was just ahead. The train was slowing to a halt. I never saw so much excitement and enthusiasm as I witnessed in this young person. He could hardly wait to tell his parents all about his new plans. God had answered my prayer to be of service to someone.

It was late when I left the train, and John was not there to pick me up. Fear and anxiety took hold, easily equivalent to what I experienced years before with Charlie. I had no cell phone, and the station closed at eleven o'clock in the evening. The time was five minutes before eleven, and my guts were in a knot. I asked the conductor if I could stay inside a little while longer because frosty air was getting into my lungs. I told him my husband was running late.

John finally arrived. The crowd at a big local game had caused traffic to detour. It therefore took John longer to arrive at the station. Then he found the border jammed with traffic. He told me he had left his place a few hours earlier. The trip usually took about one hour from start to finish, but it required three hours that night. I was praying hard, and God answered just in time.

With John living so far away, when we got together, it was almost like dating all over again. John's apartment was in a wooded area, and I liked it very much. We went to one of the auto museums and visited some local boutiques one Saturday afternoon.

That evening, we were watching television when I looked out the patio window and saw five deer looking in at us. John told me that the people who managed the complex fed the deer, even though they weren't supposed to. The apartment manager's husband worked with John and left a bag of corn for us to feed the deer. John named one Scruffy because his coat was always a mess. Another one was called Gimpy because he had suffered a broken bone in one leg and limped. I forget the other names.

The next day, only one deer was back at the door. I showed him that I was getting ready to throw the corn out to him. He left, but he came back within a few minutes with a herd of about six. The little one wanted to eat first, but he was bucked away. The big buck always ate first and then went up on the hill to keep an eye out for any danger. I found it very interesting to observe how he took care of his herd.

The weeks went by quickly, and the time came when the company decided that they wanted John to move from Michigan back to the Midwest. So, we put the condo up for sale. We called the friend who had helped us find our home. Through prayer, the condo sold within three hours.

Together, we went online to find a new home and quickly found one we liked. Two weeks later, we went to see the house and bought it.

Getting ready for the big move was complicated because we had to move our belongings across an international border. We also had to move John's furniture from Michigan at the same time, while attempting to coordinate a simultaneous arrival of both movers at the new home. The whole event turned out to be quite a production. We moved on the Fourth of July weekend. The weather was very hot and the traffic horrific. We did manage, however, to make the transition to our new home without any mishaps.

The colors in the house were not my favorites, so the first thing I did was paint the two smaller bedrooms. I then painted the kitchen and the adjoining family room. It was a big job because it had been painted a cantaloupe melon color and was a nightmare to cover.

A few weeks after the move, my sister came to visit with her friend. I was looking forward to checking out the city with my sister, a world traveler. I had no worries about getting lost. We crammed a week's worth of activities into just a few days. We went to tea rooms, shopped, and wound up exhausted. I was getting used to being in a different city. I was able to get around pretty well on my own, especially with those two experienced navigators helping me.

After they left, I felt homesick all over again, just as I had when I first moved to this state so long ago. I did have my friend Ariel. She lived about an hour away, and I was able to see her often.

Ariel had decided to have a garage sale on what turned out to be one of the hottest days of that year. Nothing was going smoothly. The day started with intense heat and humidity, which meant we had the garage door open to get some air. The weather problem escalated as people began to arrive while we were still trying to get prepared.

Many of Ariel's items were glassware. We wanted to place those items on shelves to avoid accidents. Most of them had been her mother's, and Ariel had an emotional attachment to them. Even though they hadn't seen the light of day for years, it was difficult for her to part with them.

The volatile combination of extreme heat, strangers invading before we were prepared and high emotions all combined to make us realize it was best to shut down early. Before noon we closed the garage door and went to see a movie in an air conditioned theater. All in all, it was quite an experience.

Living on my suburban street was like living with the Stepford wives. The moms would open up their garage doors. Their vans were filled with children, well behaved and sitting up oh so straight. The mothers had their makeup on just perfectly, even this early in the morning. Down went the garage doors until four o'clock; then up they would go again. When everyone was inside, down went the garage doors. You would not see or hear from them again until the repeat performance the next day.

All of the neighboring families were large, some as many as six children, most had four to five, but we hardly ever saw them outside playing. A few younger children next door had a trampoline in their backyard.

I once went out to cut the grass because I needed the exercise to keep my bones strong. I didn't have makeup on, and I wore an old T-shirt. Someone had given it to me a long time ago, and it had paint all over it. I am sure some of the neighbors took offense at the way I looked. They probably worried that I was bringing down the property values. What did I care? I was in my own yard and minding my own business, just doing a job in the heat of summer. I did not want to destroy my good tops.

I had formed a friendship with a lady across the street. She and I went to a few garage sales. One day, her car needed gas. I pointed out that there was a gas station close by. She told me she had never pumped her own gas before; she'd always had her husband do it. So I showed her how to do it. She filled up her own gas tank after that.

We also went for walks, and sometimes we would get together for a movie day. Then she found a job. For the first time since moving there, I felt like a fish out of water. Our house was beautiful, but the neighborhood was full of younger people, so I was very lonely. I did get to go to Canada to see my parents at least twice a year, which was a blessing. One time, I ventured out West to see my sisters. As I recall, that was my last time there because we all began traveling back to see our aging parents at their home.

After living in our new house for two years, we had to move. John's company had downsized. He was in middle management—an easy place for companies to trim the budget quickly. On his very last day of work, another employee resigned without any notice, leaving an inside sales position open. John asked if he could transition into that role, and his request was granted. Because the new position paid roughly a third of his previous salary, we got on our knees again and prayed that another job would come along. I also wanted to find work, and John wanted a part-time job to supplement our income. We asked our Father in heaven to help us sell our home.

The real estate agent placed his sign in the yard at seven o'clock on Sunday evening, and the house was under contract at three o'clock the following day. The house sold in record time, and we moved to a really nice luxury apartment.

A year went by, and John was doing well. He was surpassing his sales goals, earning commissions above and beyond his base salary, and we were able to live relatively comfortably.

At the beginning of the following year, the department director and the vice president of John's company met to prepare their annual departmental budget. The result was a budget projection that seemed to have no basis in the departments' past performance, the current economy, or the relative newness of the service in the marketplace. There was certainly no request for input from the sales team.

The result was an inflated projection that looked great at the corporate budget presentation. However, within the first month, sales fell drastically behind the projection, making the entire department look bad. Within months the entire sales staff was reduced to base salary and earning no commissions. With each passing month, the sales staff fell further behind their individual and group goals, making the likelihood of commission and bonus compensation nearly impossible.

Living on John's base pay and the salary from a part-time job, our income was reduced considerably but we were adjusting well. With no prospects for commissions for at least six months, John decided that it would be best to seek another employment opportunity.

We offered up more prayers to our heavenly Father, and John ended up with two part-time jobs and a new opportunity in a full-time position. We thanked God.

Feeling a little more secure, we bought a condo closer to John's new employer. We were further blessed when I found a job at an adult day care center; it was located in the church we had joined. Another blessing was that our church was very close to our home.

In my new workplace, I met a coworker who lived far out in the country, well away from the city. She invited me to her place, and we soon found a mutually convenient time to get together. When the day arrived she drove and I enjoyed the view.

As we traveled amid the rolling hills and valleys to her home, our conversations were light and fun. She came from the deep hills of Kentucky, and she was very proud of her "hillbilly" heritage. She teased me about my now being a hillbilly-in-training. Having been born Canadian, I found this just too funny. We laughed and laughed about it the entire weekend.

"Your first lesson as a 'hillbilly-in-training,'" she instructed, "is to always be on the lookout for Amish carriages. They seem to pop up out of nowhere."

"How do you do that?" I asked.

She explained that drivers have to watch out for the hot, steamy manure trail the horses leave behind on the roads. The more fresh and steamy the dropping, the closer the carriage was. Again, we just roared with laughter.

My hostess had complications from having undergone many operations, and we always seemed to be praying for one another. I prayed for her health, and she prayed for my husband and his work. So far, God has answered our prayers.

CHAPTER 12

The Walk

I HAVE ATTENDED MANY DIFFERENT educational and social events in my life: professional, secular, and Christian. I have to say that one of the most memorable experiences of my life was the Walk to Emmaus.

It is an experience of Christian spiritual renewal and formation that begins with a three-day course in Christianity. The Walk to Emmaus is a multi-denominational event that begins with an invitation from a past attendee who acts as the invitee's sponsor. My sponsor was a volunteer at my place of work and a member of our church.

The proceedings of the three-day Walk to Emmaus event are secret. This is not because they are steeped in some bizarre or weird rituals but because discussing the process would take away much of the incredibly potent opportunities for self-awareness and the fun surprises.

Because a participant cannot drive to the event, my sponsor collected me from my home and delivered me to the church. Once there, my sponsor and past participants (acting as volunteers) carried my luggage and my bedding into the church and then to my sleeping quarters while I registered at the welcome table.

Throughout the entire three days, participants were treated like royalty. We were waited on by caring volunteers (all past participants in the Walk to Emmaus) throughout our time. Once signed in, I said goodbye to my sponsor and did not see her again until the conclusion of the Walk.

The next three days were filled with self-discovery, informative talks, introductions to new friends, and more food than any human should think of consuming in a single four-day weekend. In retrospect, the Walk to Emmaus remains one of the most pleasant, spiritually enlightening, and memorable experiences of my entire life. I would recommend it to anyone without the slightest hesitation.

I believe in the power of prayer. I believe that my spirituality, my faith in a loving God allows for those prayers to be answered. One day at work, my foot was so sore that I had to drag it to get from one room to another. Crying out to Jesus, I asked him to please heal my foot so that I could work that day. After a word of prayer for help, it did stop hurting. My foot is fine to this day, thanks be to the Lord.

Christmas was coming, and John and I again decided to drive to Canada to see my parents. In late November, my dad had a massive heart attack at home. He managed to get up and refused to see a doctor or go to the hospital. A few days later, he relented and went to the hospital. He told the doctors he thought he pulled a muscle or had very bad heartburn. He wound up hospitalized for a week. For this reason, most of his children decided to go home for Christmas that year. (One of my sisters had gone home for his birthday on December seventh.) We all thought this might be his last Christmas. Dad was in his late eighties by then.

When the doctors released him from the hospital, they said there was nothing more they could do for him. Most of his arteries were blocked, and his heart would not be able to withstand an operation.

John and I arrived at Mom and Dad's home around noon on Christmas day. The first thing my mom did was hold me really tight so that she could tell me how much she loved me. Late in the day, in typical motherly fashion, she served a feast of ham, turkey, and an endless variety of side dishes.

Later on, my sister and I decided to go to our hotel for a swim. The hotel had an indoor/outdoor heated pool. Because it was snowing, it all seemed surreal—swimming in the warm water outside in the snow, but it was fun. We had invited Mom. However, she wanted to get rested for the next day.

About two hours later, my sister went back to our parents' house for the night. It seemed John and I had just fallen asleep in our hotel room when a call came from my sister. She told me to get dressed; our mom had been taken by ambulance to the hospital. I was in shock.

When we arrived at the hospital, the doctor told us she'd had a stroke, but she didn't seem to be badly affected. I believed the doctor because Mom walked herself into the ambulance and had the good sense to go right to the hospital as soon as she recognized the trouble.

I asked the doctor if we should stay, and he advised us to go back to Dad because he was still on the mend. The doctor said that Mom needed her rest; with us there, all she wanted to do was sit up and visit.

On our way back to the hotel, our car hit an icy patch and went off the road. People stopped and helped us get back on the road, and I said to my sister, "Let's go back to Mom." Thinking of our dad, however, we continued on our way.

At around 6:35 a.m. the next morning we received a call from the hospital informing us, "Your mom is not doing well. You'd better come now." I knew it was the end; I had woken up around two in the morning and prayed to our heavenly Father, "If this is your will, then let her go home."

Mom had told me a few weeks before that she wanted to go because she was really tired. I later found out her illness stemmed from a weak heart. Parents who keep secrets have no idea how much discovering the truth hurts. Every bit of knowledge can help in diagnosing and treating hereditary disorders.

When I arrived at the hospital, Mom had just died. I took my Bible (NIV) and prayed the twenty-third Psalm aloud:

> The Lord is my shepherd, I shall not want.
> He makes me lie down in green pastures.
> He leads me beside quiet waters.
> He restores my soul;
> He guides me in the paths of righteousness
> for His name sake.

My sister asked me to stop because she was having trouble dealing with Mom's death. We were all prepared to lose Dad (who had so recently had a massive heart attack). But Mom's passing was an unexpected shock. Less than twenty-four hours earlier, Mom had been bustling about the kitchen, as she had every day of our lives. John went to give our dad the news, and my sister and I had to call the rest of the family.

Concurrently, there was another death in our home town. The day before my mom's passing, the mother of my very good friend Carissa died. Because both funerals were to be held at the same church, we had to wait for the sanctuary to be available after Carissa's mother's funeral.

The day of my mom's funeral remains a blur, but John was there for me and for our family. He sang "Amazing Grace," solo and unaccompanied, from the choir loft. The flowers from the funeral of my friend's mom were left at the church for our family. What a special gift that was from their family to ours; the blossoms added so much to the atmosphere. Words cannot convey enough my gratitude to Carissa.

Since it was Christmas, the church was decorated with a huge tree full of angels. Up from the altar, the eaves were decorated with paper doves—all the things our mother loved most. How special it all was.

Driving home in winter was not the happiest of experiences. On Monday, John went to work and later returned with devastating news. He, along with 5,000 other people, had lost his job. Due to a downturn in the economy, the company had announced a major lay-off. He had been with them for five years. I wondered what could happen next. I had not even had one full day at home to grieve my mom's death. We found ourselves on our knees yet again.

I asked God not to let history repeat itself, especially when I go home at Christmas each year. I don't think that anything will ever compare to the tragedies of those two weeks in 2007 and 2008. Talk about the wind being knocked out of our sails!

John looked for work in one of the worst economies since the Great Depression. But somehow, life went on.

At work one day, there was talk about a homeless man living in his car on church property. The police were arriving within the hour to get him. As I was telling John this, he got up off the sofa so fast that I had to ask him where he was going. He said, "Let's go get him." I was in shock! John had never wanted a boarder in our home.

When we arrived at the church parking lot, we easily found the man. I asked him if he was aware of what was happening, and he wasn't. We told him the police would soon be there, and he needed to leave the church grounds. John told him to follow us, and we would give him his own bedroom and bathroom until he could get back on his feet.

The homeless gentleman was reluctant at first, but he came and stayed with us for at least three months. We received objections from friends and family; they asked us how we could be confident that he would not steal from us. My answer was that we trusted in our heavenly Father.

Although there was no theft in our home, there were a few other problems. But they were nothing we couldn't handle. I do hope someday he will find a church home and that he will find Jesus.

Before the layoff, John had won a substantial workplace prize: a new double-oven gas range. However, we thought that since he was no longer employed, the prize might be forfeited. Before New Year's, John got a call to say the range he had won was being delivered on Friday, New Year's Eve.

Then in May, another call came saying the prize he had selected was being delivered. John told the caller we had already received the range and that this must be a mistake. However, there was no way to stop it because the prize was coming the next day.

John called his old boss who was still employed, to tell him what had happened; in turn, his boss called upper management. We were instructed to keep the second range. His old boss then told John that two jobs were opening up and to watch the posting board. John responded as soon as the jobs were posted. He was offered his choice of the two positions and started back to work before the end of the month. If my husband had not been honest about the range, I am certain that he would not have learned about the job openings.

I know prayers work. I can't count how many times we have been on our knees, and our heavenly Father has listened when the request was for an honest need and not a mere want.

The new job took John from the Midwest to the Gulf Coast, so it was time to move once again. We had chosen a home specifically with the hope of retiring there. During the time that John was off work, he put down hardwood floors throughout the entire condo with the exception of the tiled bathrooms. A lot of time and money went into that project, but the renovation did pay off in the end. The house sold, but the only way it did so was through a short sale. Compared to others going through similar circumstances we lost practically nothing.

Since housing prices had plummeted in those hard times, we were very thankful. We were separated for six months, waiting for this sale. John had found a great new church down south, and I still attended our home church. Both church families prayed many prayers on our behalf, and I was able to join my husband just before Thanksgiving. We spent thousands of dollars on the move, but we finally got settled. For how long, no one could know.

Christmas was approaching. Once again, I went home to see my dad, my son, and my grandson. There was talk at John's work about streamlining, which meant another downsizing. On the plane ride to Canada, I prayed to our dear heavenly Father for help with Dad's health and John's job. Three years have passed since my dad's heart attack, and he is still living a good life. Thank you, God.

Two days after I returned home and was traveling with John, a call came through saying that John still had a job. Prayers work when it is God's will. He would have to move, however, to a central location within his territory, about an hour from where we had settled. Frustrated with this, John again looked for work and almost immediately was referred to a great job that he enjoys. Our fingers and toes are crossed that he might retire in seven years' time.

I became very involved with our new church home and joined a prayer team and a singing team that visits nursing homes. I found visiting shut-ins to be very gratifying; call it giving back.

I also looked into volunteering at a hospice organization where I began to help with fundraisers and went to see people in their homes when needed. I have taken spiritual, bereavement, and other related classes to qualify and prepare for this ministry of spending time with the dying in their final hours.

The program is called The Eleventh Hour. Volunteers are asked to sit with the dying, especially when there are no family members or relatives who can be there. It is a great service, knowing that loved ones will not be alone at this trying time. Hospice services give comfort to the family and to the person facing the end of his or her life.

The service is available almost everywhere. (If you are interested, check out the hospice services in the city in which you live.) Typically, hospice organizations are nonprofit companies. The services are facilitated by a paid staff of professionals who, in turn, train volunteers.

Help is available if needed, despite financial circumstances. Hospice organizations provide informative booklets describing their mission and activities. If anyone is faced with the knowledge of impending death, hospice services are definitely worth exploring. Some of the services offered are listed below.

- Assistance with health issues that come with aging adults.
- Doctors on call 24/7 (with permission of the patient's doctor).
- Prescription services. If the patient's medications run out and their primary care physician's office is closed (with just an answering service responding), hours may elapse before a prescription is filled. Hospice services can acquire the necessary medications within half an hour or less.
- A bereavement day camp to help children through grief and help them achieve a healthy recovery.

I encourage anyone facing this difficult time of impending loss to go online and check out the helpful services available through hospice organizations. At this stage in my life, I find that serving people with this type of need is a true blessing. As I said earlier, I call it giving back.

Epilogue

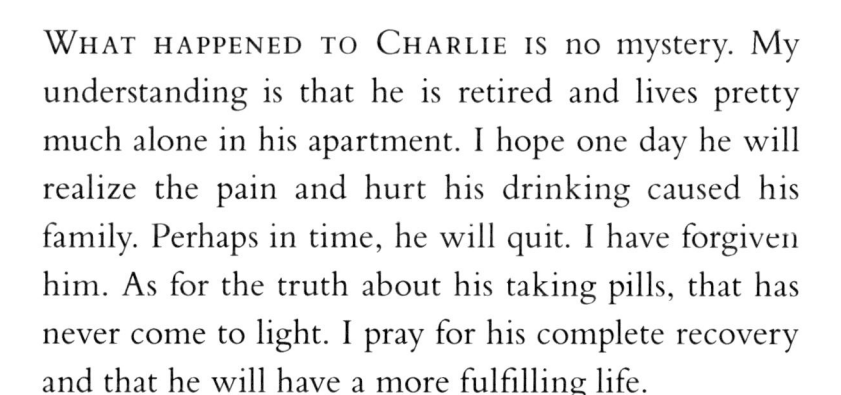

What happened to Charlie is no mystery. My understanding is that he is retired and lives pretty much alone in his apartment. I hope one day he will realize the pain and hurt his drinking caused his family. Perhaps in time, he will quit. I have forgiven him. As for the truth about his taking pills, that has never come to light. I pray for his complete recovery and that he will have a more fulfilling life.

Mulligan lives outside the city. He is an adult education instructor and is doing great in his field. I am so proud of his successful career. He is with a wonderful woman who is beautiful and has a strong character. They complement each other. Many people love him, especially his mom. I am thankful to Jesus for answering my cry for help during my son's challenging teenage years.

Without John's encouragement and support, I would never have started this book. I am not a writer, but all good things are possible through Jesus Christ.

Well, what are John's plans? We know his purpose is still in the making. Our Father in heaven isn't done with him yet.

My longtime friend Marley is retired and receiving her Canadian pension. She loves her time off, so she is able to dabble in one of her passions: decorating. Being very "artsy," she has made her place unique. Too bad she didn't go into decorating as her profession earlier in life. She has a talent that was almost wasted.

Casey, my friend from grade school, is also retired. Unfortunately, her retirement started out with a knee injury. She is enjoying her time off and spends it with her husband and her dog at their home on the water.

Ariel, a friend from the Midwest, is a night nurse, but she is taking a short personal leave while she cares for her ailing mom. Her son is now a tall, handsome young man who has a very good career; he helps his mom out in many ways. Ariel is still saddened over the loss of her dear horse, Sweet Pea, but she realizes Sweet Pea is now free of pain and suffering.

Carissa, my childhood friend, is also retired due to downsizing. She is looking for work, but in this troubled economy and in a small town that can offer only limited opportunities even in the best of times, it could be quite a challenge.

As for me, I am at an intermission in my life. I miss the personal interaction of working with clients. I had become friends with my most recent boss and miss the great outings we had together. I miss all the staff and the clients I worked with over the years.

Having moved to an area with little available work, I am using my time to write this book in gratitude to my Father in heaven.

I write these final words while sitting under a huge oak tree, the sun to my back, watching dogs chase each other into the water. The venue is a community park with a doggy play area and a community center that hosts a variety of senior events throughout the week. Waiting to go inside the community center building to call out bingo for the seniors, I say to myself: *What a great place to put my thinking cap on and write down my thoughts.*

I will leave you now with a song I received one night. I awoke but could not get back to sleep. After several hours of fitful rest, I obeyed my inner impulse, got out of bed, and headed for the living room with pen and paper in hand. When I wrote the words down, they were coming so fast. Had I not started writing on the pad—trying to remember everything—it would have been impossible to finish.

At first, I was not sure what the song was about. After reading it, the idea became very clear to me. It is about Revelations and the second coming of Christ.

In the Spirit

We are walking and talking
In the spirit of his word.
Jesus is coming
In the name of the Lord.
Trumpets are sounding
In four corners of the world.
Jesus is coming
In the name of the Lord.

We are walking and talking
In the spirit of his word.
Jesus is coming
In the name of the Lord.
He is riding his great horse
With his armor and sword.
Jesus is coming
In the name of the Lord.

We are walking and talking
In the spirit of his word.
Jesus is coming
In the name of the Lord.
With his message in spirit,
He is taking us home.
Jesus is coming
In the name of the Lord.

We are walking and talking
In the spirit of his word.
Jesus is coming
In the name of the Lord.
We'll all be resurrected
When it is his time.
Jesus is coming
To take us home.
Jesus is coming
In the name of the Lord.

Afterword

THIS BOOK IS BASED ON the facts of my life to the best of my recollection. Names and places have been altered. If any of the mentioned names are familiar, no offense is intended; it is pure coincidence.

This book is dedicated to my mom. I was quite young when, one year at Christmas, she took me by the hand and showed me a very large porcelain statue of Jesus Christ lying in a manger on a bed of straw. Thank you, Mom. She has been deceased since December 26, 2008. We all miss and love her very much.

To my loving husband, John, my heartfelt thanks. He has put up with my moods, skipped meals, edited, encouraged, and supported me throughout the creation of this book.

To my sisters, my brother, and our dad: thank you for your loving care and for everything else.

To the rest of my family and friends I have known through the years, thank you for being there for me. May God bless each one of you.

To Alex, I thank you so much for the inspiration and encouragement to plant the seed of an idea and finish this book. Without you, it would still be an outline sitting in the computer, waiting to be deleted.

To Dee, thank you for helping me find Linda so that together we could let our readers know there is a God, and he does answer prayers.

To Linda, my first editor, no words can describe the kindness, compassion, and patience you have shown me. You are a gift from God, sent to help me on this journey. Many thanks to you.

To Marian Green, my second editor, thank you for taking up the bigger challenge of fine-editing and content review. Since agreeing to take on that responsibility, these are some of the things she experienced:

- A flu or virus had her bedridden for a week and settled in her ear (which began to bleed).
- She got glass shards in her eye.
- Visiting her nephew, she inadvertently left the manuscript on her bed. Her nephew's

sister-in-law stripped the bed and washed the sheets and 100 (or more) pages of the original manuscript.
- She tripped in her garden. As she fell, her leg impaled on the grounding rod for her home. The wound required several stitches and caused a lot of pain.
- An ovarian tumor erupted.
- While swerving to avoid a car that had run a red light, she slammed on the brake, spun out, and suffered whiplash.

It would almost seem as though *someone* did not want this story to be told. But through a lot of prayer, she survived these trials.

Thanks again to all my close friends, and especially to my fellow church members, for their prayers.

Prior to completing this story of my life, my father, my brother, and Casey's husband all passed away. With thanksgiving, I pray that God has welcomed them all into his greater comfort.

Most recently, Charlie suffered a serious heart attack that required transport to a hospital via helicopter and emergency triple bypass surgery. When Mulligan informed me of this event, I prayed that the Lord's healing hand would be upon Charlie. He indeed survived and is doing well. We are all hoping that he will take up residence in the same town where Mulligan, his loving partner, and their children reside.

To Archway Publishing from Simon and Schuster, my sincerest thanks for all of your help along my journey to publication.

CPSIA information can be obtained at www.ICGtesting.com
Printed in the USA
LVOW08s2225160816

500680LV00001B/89/P